Shaker Spirits
Shaker Ghosts

Thomas Lee Freese

4880 Lower Valley Road • Atglen, PA 19310

Dedication

I dedicate this, my eighth published book and second book to address the topic of Shaker spirits, to all those who humbly seek to find God in their hearts, in Universal Mind, in the eyes of their fellow mortals, in the animal, nature, and mineral kingdoms, and in the mystery of immediate and ongoing revelation as given through Grace to their seeking souls.

In addition, I dedicate this book to all those who love the Shaker way, who sing and dance as Followers of the Lamb. May many more move beyond the admiration of a Shaker-made chair or box to find the Living Spirit of the Universal Father in all things, great and small.

Ouija is a trademark of Parker Bros. Games
Photos by author unless otherwise noted

Back cover: Photo of Thomas Freese *Courtesy of the Kentucky Arts Council*
Front cover: Photo of Pleasant Hill Meeting House by Bruce Waters

Schiffer Books are available at special discounts for bulk purchases for sales promotions or premiums. Special editions, including personalized covers, corporate imprints, and excerpts can be created in large quantities for special needs. For more information contact the publisher:

Published by Schiffer Publishing, Ltd.
4880 Lower Valley Road
Atglen, PA 19310
Phone: (610) 593-1777; Fax: (610) 593-2002
E-mail: Info@schifferbooks.com

For the largest selection of fine reference books on this and related subjects,
please visit our website at **www.schifferbooks.com**
We are always looking for people to write books on new and related subjects.
If you have an idea for a book, please contact us at
proposals@schifferbooks.com

This book may be purchased from the publisher.
Please try your bookstore first.
You may write for a free catalog.

In Europe, Schiffer books are distributed by
Bushwood Books
6 Marksbury Ave.
Kew Gardens
Surrey TW9 4JF England
Phone: 44 (0) 20 8392 8585; Fax: 44 (0) 20 8392 9876
E-mail: info@bushwoodbooks.co.uk
Website: www.bushwoodbooks.co.uk

Copyright © 2012 by Thomas Lee Freese
Library of Congress Control Number: 2012939021

Designed by Mark David Bowyer
Type set in John Handy LET / Zurich BT

ISBN: 978-0-7643-3989-9
Printed in China

Contents

Contents

My Thanks

Friends who encouraged me to write this book of Shaker ghost stories may not have realized how their support was valued. These friends include: Randy Folger, Mary Brinkman, Normandi Ellis, Sarah Thomas, all of the Pleasant Hill Singers, Rose Sorrell, Don Pelly, the administration and employees of Shakertown, and the visitors to Pleasant Hill—those who shared their ghost stories. I am grateful to the Pleasant Hill Trustees and all who worked in small and large ways to restore Shakertown and provide a haven for learning, meditation and insight. Thanks to Dena Sollano for technical help in the home stretch, for the original book version. Thanks also to all the folks who shared their stories for the second version of *Shaker Ghosts,* and to folks involved with the White Water Shaker village who were supportive in hearing my stories from Pleasant Hill and in sharing some tales from the Shaker village there in Ohio. Thanks to Carol Medlicott for her wisdom and research, providing valuable perspective through the interview.

Thanks also goes to the psychics who provided additional information and to the Friends of White Water for historical background on that village.

I also thank the Shakers. Their hard work and vision provided a number of sturdy nineteenth-century villages of exceptional construction. Their many manuscripts of original songs continue to provide joy and inspiration for those open to breathing their words into songs of praise. And their example of simple lives of service gives us hope when we are bounced around by a busy world.

Lower road looking west, Shakertown at Pleasant Hill. *Photo by Thomas Freese.*

Introduction

The best stories of ghosts, spirits, and angels are true tales related in first person. I have collected primary-source ghost stories since the mid-1990s. The majority of the ghost stories I hear come from folks I meet. As the tellers speak into the microphone to record their stories, I can look into their eyes, see the effect of their encounter, and feel, secondhand, their emotions as they heard, saw, or felt something from the other side. When I was a volunteer singer at Pleasant Hill, I heard many stories of the active Shaker spirits there and I collected those tales in 1998 and published them in 2005.

In the passage of time since *Shaker Ghost Stories from Pleasant Hill, Kentucky* has been circulating and read by many, I have heard additional ghost stories from both Pleasant Hill, near Harrodsburg, Kentucky, and also tales from the historic Shaker community of White Water, in Ohio. I decided to recreate the original book, adding new stories and photographs. I also wanted to add material I had gathered for the first version of *Shaker Ghost Stories* but that were not included for various reasons. As I travel to book fairs and perform as a professional storyteller, I still hear folks tell more stories of spirit encounters at Pleasant Hill, stories which should be added. And thus a new and updated version of *Shaker Ghost Stories* was born to provide more stories, photographs and tales from another Shaker village. In *Shaker Spirits Shaker Ghosts* I have updated, to the best of my knowledge, information about the people and places mentioned in the original book. For instance, the original book had sixty contributors, and as of this writing, five have passed on to the spirit world.

Centre Family Dwelling, Pleasant Hill. *Photo by Thomas Freese.*

I also here provide a wider view of what the manifestation of discarnate spirits, including deceased Shaker brethren, meant to the Shakers. I consulted with Professor Carol Medlicott of Northern Kentucky University, who had much experience studying the Shaker journals and was able to provide a perspective on the Shakers' view of communicating with the spirits of those who died in physical terms, but were alive in spirit. Since those early days, in the latter 1990s, I also came into contact with The Western Shaker Study Group, who graciously invited me to give talks about the *Shaker Ghosts* at the Union Village Shaker building, which had become home to Otterbein Retirement Community. I traveled to Watervliet, and in discussions with a number of folks, heard of active Shaker spirits at those historic locations. Since I didn't feel that the material from the Ohio Shaker villages was sufficient to create a book, I decided to combine that new material with the updated version.

To summarize, this new version of *Shaker Ghosts* includes:

- The complete set of original stories from the first version of *Shaker Ghosts*,
- New stories, gathered since 1998, from Shakertown at Pleasant Hill,
- Ghost stories from other Shaker villages,
- Additional photographs,
- Reports from ghost hunter investigations at Pleasant Hill,
- Previously unpublished material from the original research and interviews conducted at Pleasant Hill,
- An interview with Shaker scholar Carol Medlicott,
- More information concerning the Shakers spirituality,
- Bibliography of books utilized and recommended reading,
- Shaker ghost stories from online postings, and,
- Several walking interviews with psychics who visited Shakertown at Pleasant Hill, in Kentucky and White Water, in Ohio.

In general, the new material is blended into the original text.

I came to know Pleasant Hill, in 1990, as a visitor and tourist. At that time, I was living in Santa Fe, New Mexico, and traveling in the eastern half of the United States. I was looking for a new home after having lived in Santa Fe for eleven years. Shakertown was one of the drawing forces that led me to move to the nearby bluegrass area, Lexington, Kentucky. It was then that I became aware of Shakertown being an oasis of rural land and nineteenth-century history, quaint and quiet.

But it wasn't until a friend invited me to a nature walk and talk at Shakertown, and afterwards I heard and joined the Pleasant Hill Singers, that I came to know the magnetic pull of peacefulness and spirituality that is the core of the Shaker experience. Some of the singers are also employees at Shakertown and those seasoned workers used that exact term, "Shaker experience," to describe the initiatory and direct encounter with the Shaker spirits. I was truly mesmerized by the accounts of active spirit presence at Pleasant Hill, and it seemed a sacred duty to hear those stories and to take it as a personal mission to record them.

I feel that the hallmark of a true ghost story is its simplicity. They may be odd, perhaps, but oftentimes, the encounter is no more than hearing a voice, smelling a fragrance, or seeing a glimpse of a Shaker figure. And there is hardly a visit to Shakertown that is without an updated account of a friend or guest or fellow Shaker singer having had another Shaker experience. Nearly all of the stories I've heard involve Shaker spirits true to their collective character displayed in life—helpful, inspired, and dedicating their lives to God and service to others.

I am accepting of the reality of ghosts and spirits. I already was a believer when, at age 40, I joined the Shaker singers. I have countless times, since childhood, experienced the presence of ghosts and I once saw one. My mental inclination is to believe in ghosts, faeries, psychic phenomenon, and much more. Thus, in a sense, I don't really need the direct spirit encounter; I am pleased to hear others tell their tales which verifies my notion of reality. I have a collection of ghost stories from the world outside of Pleasant Hill, too. I believe that the entire world and any and every household can be visited by spirits. Ghosts carry their mortal personalities onward through the death experience. Their post-transition character and actions are compatible with their pre-death inclinations and predisposition. Thus, some ghosts may play out their drama of fear or territorial defensiveness. Other spirits may linger and be a source of love and support. But you don't get a personality makeover. If, when you cross over, you are sad and depressed, then that emotional theme is carried over into the spirit realm. If, when alive, you were pleasant and cheerful, then you'll be a pleasant and cheerful spirit. I detail some of my experiences with the Other World in my other ghost story books.

Shakertown interpreters crossing the village lane.
Photo by Thomas Freese.

I believe that the communication and behavior of ghosts is purposeful. They show an intention to gift a visit to a certain person for a certain reason at a certain time in a certain manner. I've found this true in ghostly encounters anywhere, including Shakertown. We all feel their presence, some of us see and hear them, and they have a reason for creating the encounter...if nothing else than to say, "I am here, I am real, I have something to say or share." Those of you who have heard stories of families with haunted houses also know that the interactions of the relationships between the living and the living-in-spirit can be every bit as layered, humorous, and testy as those we experience with our friends and family. Ghosts utilize symbolic communication, metaphor, and humor. And the relationship, living to ghost, is just as negotiable as relationships among the living. That is, if your teenager is playing the music too loud, and you've had enough, you might shout, "Turn that down!" And most of the time, the child will turn down the music. It's the same with folks who live with ghosts, as they shout, "Stop playing with the lights" or "Leave my dog alone" and "Get out of the bathroom—this is my private time!"

The *Course in Miracles* states that we teach what we have learned. I believe that the spirits are encouraging us to keep an open mind and open heart. They have made the life transition into pure spirit. The expansive universe begins in our own mind, and the reminders to our own spirit essence may be little, subtle things along the way. If you have had spirit encounters, then you know and understand. If you haven't yet seen, heard, or felt a ghost, then just keep an open mind and heart to believe others when they say that they heard a ghost singing in the Meeting House when "nobody" was there.

North Lot ruins, Pleasant Hill. *Photo by Thomas Freese.*

The Shakers at Pleasant Hill, Kentucky

I had no idea of the extensive history of the spiritual community known as the Shakers, and many people have very limited knowledge, if any, of them. Some of that limited information may be skewed to view only their celibacy as their downfall. The standard joke goes: "The Shakers died out because they were celibate." But celibacy does not fully explain their increase from 6 to 6,000 members, or their later decline. True, each Shaker was naturally born of a woman, yet they claimed, for their heavenly destination, to be "worthy of the resurrection of the dead," that they must "live as angels." Often, Matthew 22:30 is cited. At any rate, the Shakers prospered, thrived, and their commitment to non-sexual relations was but one facet of a deep love for life, God, and their fellow mortals. When visiting Shakertown, and despite the material evidence of industry and labor, it nevertheless takes a certain amount of imagination and investigation to see just how successful the Shakers were in living-right livelihood, creating harmony of spirit and body, and implementing social and gender justice.

At the time of the Shakers, not all the folks who lived near them, or who had contact with them, or who came after them were respectful of their faith or their different ways. Early Shakers were at times beaten, harassed, ostracized, and, as noted below in a recent press release from South Union Shaker Village, Kentucky, rejected entirely even after their deaths.

Back in 1922, when the Shaker village at South Union closed, a public auction was held to divide and sell the community's 4,000-acre farm into smaller tracts. One of the largest tracts included over twenty-five buildings that had once been part of the village. It also included a cemetery. The new owner of this large tract first destroyed the 1847 East House, one of the Shakers' four communal dwellings, recently damaged by a tornado. Next, he razed the 1818 Meeting House and built on its site a brick home for use by his family on weekends. Other buildings followed until attention was turned to the village cemetery. Oral historical accounts relay that the fence surrounding the six-acre graveyard was removed and the stone markers ground into lime to be used on the fields. Barns were built over part of the burying ground and the rest of it was cultivated for many years to come.

The members of the United Society of Believers in Christ's Second Appearing were from Manchester, England. Led by an uneducated, but charismatic, woman named Ann Lee, the small group of believers sailed to New York in 1774. After initial struggles, their group grew with evangelizing efforts and soon sent missionaries to spread the Shaker faith and to establish communities set apart from the world. The Shakers created nineteen utopian villages based on equality of the sexes, pacifism, and religious freedom. They particularly thrived during the first half of the nineteenth century. They believed in common ownership of property, celibacy, public confession of sins, and separation from the world.

The industrious Shakers thrived. Their motto was: "Hands to work, and hearts to God." Pleasant Hill, Kentucky was founded in 1808, and within three decades, became the third largest of the Shaker communities, with 500 members. The Civil War, shifting markets, declining membership, and inadequate leadership lead to a decline in the latter 1800s. The last Pleasant Hill Shaker passed away in 1923.

Pleasant Hill's restoration was begun in 1966. A visitor will find 33 restored buildings and some 3,000 acres of original Shaker land. A thriving historic site, Shakertown is located twenty-five miles southwest of Lexington, near the dramatic limestone palisades of the Kentucky River. The village has overnight accommodations, a craft store, farm and gardens, and a number of educational programs. The educational programs include herb classes, music programs, nature walks, Civil War encampments, draft farm animal husbandry, archaeological talks, and specialized Shaker studies. Shaker craft classes teach participants how to make nesting boxes, chairs, brooms, and rugs. Shaker interpreters wear Shaker-like garb and make brooms, weave, cook, drive wagons, make shoes, and provide Shaker song and dance in the historic Meeting House. The men are dressed in dark trousers with a vest, black or navy blue in color. Under their simple vests they wear a long-sleeved white shirt. When they are outdoors, the men don a sturdy, straw hat with a flat, oval top. The women interpreters reproduce the Shaker clothing with a blue dress and a white apron. They have a white modesty scarf that crosses the bosom and show respect with sun cap or bonnet. Some of the female singers wear a completely white dress to imitate the Shaker women's Sunday meeting attire. Both men and women wear simple black shoes without buckles.

A number of the sightings of Shaker spirits were assumed to be encounters with Pleasant Hill employees who were dressed in Shaker-style clothing. The irony is that the employees are recreating Shaker devotion to work while their Spiritual brethren, the Shaker ghosts, are active in their midst.

For several decades, I have been traveling to Mercer County, near Harrodsburg, Kentucky, to Shakertown. Even when I worked as an artist in residence and was a four-hour drive away, I was still motivated to join with the Shaker singers and be once again inspired by the Shaker music. We would talk about the Shakers; there was always some new bit of history or biography to learn about Mother Ann or the Pleasant Hill Shakers. The stories of the lives of those pioneers in land and adventurers in spirit were amazing to us. And with each singer's rehearsal or winter retreat, there were more tales to tell of the Shaker spirits. They were just as active as us! I was active with the Pleasant Hill Singers from 1996 until 2006.

Stone fence and orchard at Pleasant Hill. *Photo by Thomas Freese.*

"Are There Any Ghosts Around Here?"

The Shakers wrote over 30,000 songs and some of those tunes were written at Pleasant Hill. When I joined the Shaker singers, I found that each gathering was a chance to learn a new song, and some of those songs were very inspiring to us. The titles reveal the Shakers' devotion to love, honest living, and openness to the spirit of God moving through them: "Now's the Time to Enter In," "Since We are Called to Liberty," "Who Will Bow and Bend Like a Willow," "Pretty Love and Union," "I'll Beat my Drum," and "I'm on My Way to Zion."

Meeting House, Pleasant Hill. *Photo by Don Pelly.*

We performed in costume throughout the year, and once a year, in the winter, we had our singers' retreat. During the retreat, we wore jeans and enjoyed the relaxing atmosphere and time to become better friends. We had new singing material to learn, but on breaks and on Saturday night, we could gather around and talk about how the Shakers influenced us.

On February 11, 1997, we were in the basement of the West Lot Dwelling, gathered in couches and chairs around the cozy fire. One of the seasoned singer/employees mentioned their Shaker experience of being accompanied by a spirit presence in the village, and the stories from our group flowed along for several hours. When I expressed my interest to know more, I was given names of other Pleasant Hill workers. I was determined that the stories of Shaker ghosts not be lost.

It took another year, though, of hearing more stories and getting some encouragement from friends, to get up the courage to commit to the task of interviewing folks I didn't know. I asked and was given permission by officials at Pleasant Hill to speak with their employees about their experiences. So in the spring of 1998, I carried a tape recorder and notebook and began to follow leads, interviewing people in person or by phone to obtain their Shaker ghost stories. My search led me around the village at Pleasant Hill, to a bakery in nearby Harrodsburg, and out to various other states to contact visitors from Tennessee, California, and Ohio.

Invisible Hand Saves Worker

I was never quite sure where the ghost stories from Shakertown would pop up. I happened to be in Nicholasville, Kentucky at the Nicholasville Boot Store. As the shop owner was steaming the brim on my hat, I mentioned that I was writing a book on Shaker ghost stories. The man did not seem surprised, and actually reported an incident involving a man he knew.

His friend had been working at Shakertown for a Lexington construction and remodeling company. The shop owner's friend was working on a window and his arms were stretched up to use both hands on a tool. Neither hand was available to hold on to the window frame, as he had one leg dangling outside and the other leg inside the structure. Suddenly, he felt himself lose his balance and start to fall out of the window but an invisible hand grabbed his ankle and saved him from a disastrous fall.

East Family Dwelling

Shaker Past Life

This story was a recent addition to the collection. It may have happened in the East Family Dwelling. I was invited to give a talk about the Shaker ghost stories at a Tuesday night, weekly meditation class at the Center for Integrative Health in Louisville. This group is facilitated by Ann Lawes, Weda Reihm, and Barbara Bloecher. After I talked about the active Shaker spirits, Barbara seemed very keen to tell me what happened when she was visiting Shakertown years ago. This story brings up the fact that a number of people believe they recognize past life connections when they visit a Shaker village.

Barbara Bloecher relates:

When I was 35 years old, I was having a romance with a man. He surprised me by making arrangements for dinner and an overnight stay at Shakertown. This was late spring-early summer and happened in the late 1980s. I was really excited about going. We drove from Louisville and the first place we went into was the Gift Shop, where I saw the reproduction Shaker furniture, boxes, and all that.

We started then to walk around on our self-guided tour, going into a few buildings. Then we went into a building which was a dormitory for the Shakers. It housed the women. It was a great, big long brick building with separate steps and entrances for men and women.

When I went in, I was immediately *overcome* with grief. I felt so sad—it was despair! I kept quiet about it, not mentioning my feelings to my friend, but I wanted out of that building. We then went outside and walked around to see other buildings within the village. The more we visited, the more I got just really depressed. I was despondent. And it wasn't a feeling only from the first building we went into. I didn't have that feeling in the Gift Shop. We walked about, but the longer I stayed, the worse I felt.

I was trying to figure out, *how am I going to tell him that I'm not up for this weekend?* We had planned to stay two days and one night, returning on Sunday afternoon. While he went off to the men's restroom, I sat down on a bench. I sat there, talking to myself, trying to get myself back together. It seemed like there was a vision in front of me. I could see that the long field across from me had been, in the Shaker's time, a garden. I had been a Shaker woman and there was a Shaker man involved. It was a past life being recalled and it was right there in front of me.

I saw myself in the garden. I also saw the Shaker man and he was looking at me. As soon as I saw that look he had, I understood that we had a relationship. We were not supposed to be having that relationship. The despair from that was heartbreaking. Then I realized that he had been run off because of his relationship with me. Then I saw that I died in childbirth there at the Shaker village.

And ever since that time, I've had an aversion to anything that is Shaker (except the furniture).

My friend came out of the men's room and I told him, "I have to talk to you about this. I cannot stay here. I don't know what's wrong with me. This place makes me very sad, very uncomfortable. And it's not just a passing sadness—there is a lot of grief and loss here for me. I need to leave."

Then he replied, "Well we'll just go to dinner and then we'll go home."

I said, "No. I need to leave."

He then said, "Alright…"

I don't think I gave him specifics of my vision, but I didn't completely leave him in the dark about what I'd seen. I told him as much as I could so he would understand why I wanted to leave.

So we left right away. I've never forgotten my experience at Shakertown and I've never been back. I have sometimes thought that I might go back to see if it happens again. Now I'm not a wimpy kind of person. I've had a lot happen to me concerning the paranormal. But I've never had an experience with such sadness and such an aversion to one place and people. The only place where that sadness lifted, just a little, was in the Meeting House. Of all the buildings I went into that day, the Meeting House was where I was the least uncomfortable. I don't have a problem singing *Simple Gifts*. And it's not Shakertown; it's me. I had always thought that visiting Pleasant Hill would be a great thing to do. Before we left, I was enthusiastic—dinner and an overnight, "let's go!"

That Didn't Happen

One day, when I was taking a walk around the village with a friend, we stopped by the Cooper's Shop. Employee Connie Carlton is interesting to visit and watch make wooden buckets and tools. Connie went through the barrier gate, closing it behind him. While he walked over to the other side of the room (where he did his craft demonstrations), my friend and I watched the barrier gate again open and close. When something like that happens, our mind is only too willing to put it into our experiential/mental File 13. In other words, the rational mind simply says, "That didn't happen."

I asked Connie if he had any ghostly encounters while working at Shakertown. He told of one event that happened to him in the nearby East Family Dwelling in 1994.

I went over there one evening to use the downstairs restroom. As one comes into the first, big room, there are two doors that were left open. This happened before the Shaker Life Exhibit was set up. I was the only one in the building. As I came back out, I was walking close to the door on the left side. The door slammed shut, right behind my heels. You couldn't have grabbed it and shut it any faster. It was like something said, "You get out of here—you're on *my* turf!" It made the hair stand up on my neck. No other doors or windows were open. And there wasn't any reason for it—no gust of wind. I never would have thought about it if the door had swung around real slowly. But, it was like someone was trying to kick me out of the house. There are a lot of things you can't explain.

Phantom Footsteps

Connie was working on his cedar and sassafras wooden buckets in April 1999 when a few overnight guests asked him to help start up their car with his jumper cables. The guests were a woman from Tennessee and her adult daughter. After assisting them, the woman perhaps felt relaxed enough to ask Connie the question, "Are there any strange happenings around here?"

Dixie, Betty Jo, and Connie (left to right).
Photo by Thomas Freese.

Connie asked the woman just what she meant by "strange things" and the woman confided, "Well, like *ghosts* in the village." She then told about her stay the previous night in a room in the West Family Sister's Shop.

My daughter was asleep in her bed and I was getting ready for bed. I know that I had bolted shut our door to the hallway. I was wearing my nightgown and I was in the bathroom. The bathroom door was open just a little. While I was in the bathroom, I heard our door open. I listened as footsteps sounded across the room. Then I heard the things I had set on the bedside table being lifted up and set down, one by one.

The guest told Connie that she and her daughter ended up sleeping in the same bed that night.

East Family Sister's Shop

Bumps and Stomping

It seems that every Shaker building has had unusual occurrences. Close to the Cooper's Shop lies the East Family Sister's Shop, built in 1855. There are weaving and spinning demonstrations on the first floor; and, as in a number of the restored buildings, there are guest lodgings above. It was in the East Family Sister's Shop that some employees heard sounds in supposedly vacant rooms.

One of the interpreters tells of sounds of the loom being worked at night. Those rooms are locked at six o'clock, but people who stay in the guest rooms upstairs have often heard the sounds of the shuttle and beating board. Although there are never any employees working on the looms at night, people have heard someone slamming on the looms.

A man who has worked in maintenance for ten years at Shakertown is nicknamed "Tucker." Tucker has worked below the floorboards of the East Family Sister's Shop and he has heard "bumps and stomping."

East Family Sisters' Shop. *Photo by Thomas Freese.*

Feel A Presence

Edith Allen Ransdell worked for thirteen years in the East Family Sister's Shop. She demonstrated both spinning and weaving in two separate rooms across the hall from each other. As she went from one room to another, she would often feel a presence, perhaps a female spirit, follow her—but always stopping at the door of each room.

Lonnie E. Brown and Roberta Simpson Brown are friends of mine who like to venture out and investigate haunted and historical sites. They are both authors and fellow tellers of all kinds of stories, including ghost stories. They reported on an experience at Shakertown when they went there with another ghost hunter and author Robert Parker.

The Village is Active

We'd heard that Shakertown was haunted, so on March 24, 2006, we set out with our friend, Robert Parker (Louisville's Mr. Ghost Walker), for a springtime night of adventure and ghost hunting. Since there is no central hotel at Pleasant Hill, we were assigned rooms on the second floor of the East Family Sisters' Shop. We checked in, left our luggage, and started out exploring with our ghost-hunting equipment.

A cold rain had begun to fall, but we braved the elements and explored all the buildings that were open along the village pike. Our dowsing rods and readings on our EMF (electromagnetic field) meters indicated that we had ghostly company, but nothing materialized for us to see. The rain began coming down harder and the March wind grew cold and cutting, so we returned to our rooms and went to bed.

With the lights out, the room was in total darkness. We decided that we could create a night light if we turned on the closet light and closed the closet door. The little crack of light created the effect we wanted at first, but we soon noticed that the room was getting brighter and brighter! We looked at the closet and saw that the door was wide open! We agreed that we must not have closed it securely, so we tried again. After a couple of minutes, the room grew bright and, again, the door was open. We repeated the process of firmly closing the door several times, but it simply would not stay closed. We gave up, turned off the light, and left the door open.

As we drifted off to sleep, we became aware of a light flashing beside the bed. It was the electric clock we'd brought from home. It wasn't a digital clock, but it had a lighted face. It had never flashed like that before and it has never done so since, but that night it looked like a strobe light. Between the actions of the door and the clock, we came to the conclusion that the Shaker spirits did not want us to waste electricity!

As we started to doze off for a second time, we were jolted awake by the loud, distinctive sound of footsteps overhead. We assumed that a latecomer had come in and was occupying the room over us. We heard the footsteps off and on during the night.

The next morning as we were leaving, we told Robert about the footsteps over our room. A cleaning lady was in the hall and overheard us.

"That's not possible," she said. "Let me show you."

We followed her upstairs and watched as she opened the door. We were surprised to find that the room over us was only a small storage room! Nobody could have walked around, yet we both heard the footsteps.

After breakfast, we decided to visit the Meeting House where the Shakers held their worship services and did whirling dances. We pulled the door open, and at once, the three of us were engulfed in a strong whirlwind coming out the door. It was so strong that it raised our hair. It lasted only a moment, and then it was gone as suddenly as it had come. We thought we would get lots of readings on our equipment when we went inside, but all was calm. Nothing was caught. We must have met the spirits going out as we came in.

Are You Being Served?

I met Gloria Stanton and her husband when I was in Somerset and they hosted my talk for their writers group. I also shared many ghost stories when I stayed overnight with the Stanton's. Gloria told me about an experience at Shakertown.

My husband, Oris, and I moved to Pulaski County in 1991 from upstate, New York. He had taken early retirement from Eastman Kodak and took a job with Somerset Community College teaching chemistry. I established a class through Community Education teaching English as a Second Language.

In about 1996, we visited Shaker Village and spent the night at the Sister's House. I'm not sure if it was the East or West Family Dwelling. I remember the room as it seemed comparatively large, and we had single beds. I believe one of them was a trundle bed. At about the crack of dawn, I sat up directly in bed in a cold sweat as a figure—a slightly plump woman, but not short—dressed in period clothing with a white bonnet, full white apron, and long dress swept into the room carrying an oval, silver-colored tray in both hands. I believe there were dark grapes on the tray.

"Where should I put this?" she asked, continuing to walk past me.

I was dumbstruck and didn't answer her. She disappeared then. My husband, a deep sleeper, missed the whole thing. However, he has enjoyed telling people about it over the years, not in jest, either. He knows that I was a picture of pale fright when I woke him up. I realize this, what we call "a vision" probably took just a minute, but the details of it had a lasting effect on me. I really would not consider staying overnight there again.

Until I read Thomas' book, *Shaker Ghost Stories from Pleasant Hill*, I thought I was alone in my "encounter" experience at Shaker Village. I think I have a slightly higher perception, or awareness. [As I said] my husband has enjoyed telling my story to others, but I don't think he doubts what happened either.

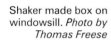

Shaker made box on windowsill. *Photo by Thomas Freese*

East Family Brethren's Shop

Rose Sorrell, once the co-owner of the Harrodsburg Bakery, started working at Shakertown when she was fifteen years old. She worked in the gift shop, which was first housed in the Farm Deacon's Shop. After she'd worked there for two years, the gift shop was moved to its present location in the Carpenter's Shop. On a lovely summer's day in 1998, I drove the ten minute drive from Shakertown to meet Rose and hear her Shaker ghost stories. Rose is a friendly soul and encouraged me to keep collecting the stories. She helped by giving me more names of those she knew who had had Shaker experiences.

Rose Sorrell told of a time when a third-shift maintenance worker was at the East Family Brethren's Shop. The East Family Brethren's Shop is located in the east part of the village. The Shaker community of Pleasant Hill was divided into five communal families and each family had its own dwellings and shops. For example, there is the Centre Family, the East Family, and the West Family Dwellings, etc.

The worker was trying to help two guests get into the building. The exterior door simply has a latch to lift up and is not locked. He could not budge the latch, and he even tried to leverage it open with a crowbar. Some guests, upstairs, heard the sounds and came downstairs. They opened the door from the inside with no problem.

Tanyard Brick Shop

Ghost Opens Door

One former employee of Shakertown tells about Lee Releford, a man who once worked for the housekeeping department at Pleasant Hill. He went every day to the Tanyard Brick Shop, just down the hill from the East Family Brethren's Shop, to pick up the linen. When putting his key in the door, the door did not open. He felt that he needed to ask permission, saying: "Okay, can I come in?" Then he'd turn the key, and the door would open. He said that this happened every time he went down there, and it *only* happened to him. When another Pleasant Hill employee took his key there one day, they were able to open the door without any difficulty.

One day, one of the Pleasant Hill maintenance workers and a few other men drove to the Tanyard Brick Shop to do work on the second floor. They entered a vacant building, as there were no guests staying in the rooms at that time and no other vehicles were parked outside. From their vantage point in the second-floor room, and with all the windows on that floor, they would have seen or heard a visitor coming into the Tanyard. They saw no visitors or other workers, but when they came back downstairs, they were surprised to find a log in the middle of the floor.

Heavy Breathing at Shakertown

The following story comes from Naomi Applegate.

I believe it was the summer of 1980 when I had occasion to visit Pleasant Hill, Kentucky. I did not know much about the Shaker community other than their accomplishments and, of course, their famous furniture style. I was aware that, as a part of their religion, they were celibate and worshiped in a fashion that caused people to call them Shakers.

My parents came to visit my family in Kentucky where we had recently moved. A few days after arriving, my mother expressed a wish to visit and stay at Pleasant Hill. I had just heard that there was a three-month waiting list to stay overnight there. I was certain we would not be able to stay the night, but after much prodding, I contacted a concierge there and was shocked to learn we could stay at The Tanyard due to the size of our party. One of the benefactors of Pleasant Hill used this building and allowed guests occasionally. We made our reservation.

My mother, father, brother, my two young sons, and I went to visit Pleasant Hill. My husband was coming down later that night after work to stay with us. When we arrived, we checked in and drove to the Tanyard which is located a distance from the main village area. I remember a yard area with a dry-stack wall around. The building sat back a bit from the wall and no trees were near the front of the building. It has been a long time, but in my distant memory, I believe the lower floor was mainly a large room. On the right, against the wall, was a staircase to the second floor with a hallway running to the left past a bedroom and bath, then left to go along a short hall into another bedroom with a bath. The second bedroom containing two beds is where my family slept. My parents were in the first bedroom and my brother slept downstairs on the couch.

My husband arrived very late that night and went straight to bed. He and my oldest son slept in one bed and I slept with my youngest son in the other. I could not go to sleep and went into our bathroom to finish reading a book I had taken from the bookcase downstairs. I sat sideways on the commode with my left side to the pipes running up the wall and my back to a window in the wall immediately to the right side of the commode.

The Tanyard, Shakertown at Pleasant Hill. *Photo by Thomas Freese.*

I had been reading the book for some time. It wasn't a particularly interesting story line and I remember thinking, "Perhaps it will get better..." I kept reading. I slowly became aware of a sighing sound nearby. I thought perhaps it was the plumbing behind the commode. Then I thought it was tree branches against the building or window. I looked out the window and there were no trees on that side near the building. I went back to the book.

Shortly afterwards, I heard the sound again, but it was louder and closer. My first thought was that it sounded like the breathing of an asthmatic person. I got up and walked around the house thinking perhaps a family member had gotten up. No. I was the only person awake. I went back to the book determined to finish before we left in the morning.

As I returned to the book, I suddenly felt air moving beside the right side of my face and again heard the breathing. This time, however, it was very pronounced, heavy breathing. With each unseen exhaled breath, air moved past my face.

I jumped up and ran out of the bathroom, slamming the door closed, and quickly sat on my bed next to my son. My heart was hammering! I told myself that I certainly was imagining the sound and moving air.

Then I noticed the light shining out from under the bathroom door. This door was a heavy door made of thick vertical wood slabs with another heavy piece of wood placed diagonally across it. There was a gap of an inch or two at the bottom of the door. I could still hear the noise moving to and fro in the bathroom. I was terrified! I knew without a doubt that whatever was in that bathroom was going to be coming out into the bedroom.

I am a "double" preacher's kid. My mother and father were both ordained ministers. I did the only thing I could think to do. I said aloud, "I plead the protection of the blood of Jesus Christ over this house and everyone in it."

The sound of heavy breathing and movement immediately ceased.

Now I was REALLY frightened. I sat awake in the middle of that bed the rest of the night, making sure nothing would hurt my children.

The next day I learned about the Shaker belief that they could communicate with their dead. I couldn't wait to leave Shakertown. I have been back to visit one time—unwillingly. I will never, ever stay in Pleasant Hill again.

I did not tell anyone about the experience for a very long time. Partially because I did not want to talk about it, but also because having this unexplained experience is, well, it's just a tad bizarre.

About seven years later I took a friend to a psychic for her birthday at her request. I had never heard of this woman, but she had done readings for my friend's mother for years. She was not a professional and did readings only for friends or their friends. I had no intention of having a reading myself. I am definitely a skeptic. We went to this woman's home and she took my friend to another room.

After some time they finished. I told the woman I was not interested; I had simply accompanied my friend. When pressed, I let her know I really did not believe there are many true psychics around. She gave me a long look. Then she said to me, "You had a paranormal experience in the past. It was quite unpleasant and frightened you a lot. It was a man. He was very hostile and meant you harm." I was floored! I had never told my friend about my experience at Pleasant Hill. I have to believe this woman had real psychic ability.

A few years after my experience at the Tanyard, I wrote to Pleasant Hill asking if anyone had reported paranormal experiences at their site. I received a lovely letter saying that there were no reports of such happenings and hopefully I had had a lovely stay. I got quite a chuckle at myself to have expected anything different.

Haunted Honeymoon

The following comes from Kylie Jude.

We recently got married, and for our honeymoon, we went to the Pleasant Hill Shaker Village here in Kentucky, which is where we got engaged, so it was cool to be back there. We stayed two nights in the Tanyard, which was a big house off to itself. We soon discovered that our honeymoon suite was haunted.

It's a long story, but basically, there was a little boy following us around, and possibly a female in her twenties. This information was picked up through visions and voices, though, and cannot technically be proven. Not yet, anyway.

There were a couple incidents that we can't explain away, like on Saturday, Eric got a book out of the bookshelf downstairs, and brought it into one of the bedrooms while I took a little nap. The book was called *Ghost Towns*. He flipped through it for a while, and then one of the electric candle lights—the lights that look like candles—started flickering. So he got up and tightened the bulb and it quit. Then he sat back down and started reading again, and the same bulb started flickering again.

Finally, he said "Will you please stop it?"

Immediately, the light stopped flickering and burned bright without any more problems.

Then, when he was done with the book, he wanted to bring it into the bedroom where we were sleeping, but I told him not to because I got bad vibes from it. He took the book back downstairs and put it back in the book case. Then we went to bed, and he fell asleep, but I lay awake for hours. I just couldn't sleep. I started seeing and hearing strange things, so I turned the light on. He woke up, and we were up from around 2-4 a.m. We ended up in the kitchen downstairs, just smoking and talking and eating. Some more noises occurred at 3:16 a.m., but didn't last very long. Then we came back to bed at 4, and finally went to sleep.

The next morning was Sunday and our last day there. We were packing up and noticed that the same book was lying on the bed beside ours, in our room. It was wrapped up in my lingerie, like someone had put it there. Neither of us sleepwalks or anything, so it was really weird.

Then when we checked out, we told the guy who worked there that the Tanyard House was haunted, and he said he had heard the same said by others who had stayed there, and that they actually kept a journal in the book case for visitors to record their ghostly experiences in. We hadn't seen the journal, but we had both been drawn to the book case the whole time. And if Eric had put the book back in the book case after it was left it in our room, maybe he would have seen it. We think that's mainly what it wanted, but it was too late by the time we figured it all out.

We are going back someday and doing an investigation with a Paranormal Society.

Staying at the Tanyard Changed Our Lives

"Jane" contacted me after finding my first book of Shaker ghost stories. Long before that, she and her family drove for three days from south Texas to spend time at Shakertown. I interviewed her on the phone and her story seemed nearly surreal, complete with odd comments from the children, such as a question her daughter posed when they drove down the hill into the little valley where the Tanyard is located. When her daughter saw the rising lights of lightning bugs, she asked her mother, "Are those the souls of dead people?"

On the first night, Jane *thought* she heard her husband checking on the kids in their separate room, hearing footsteps and the floor creaking and the door to their room being swung open. She closed it four times that night.

She heard running water, and thought that her husband, not being able to sleep, was doing the dishes. Despite the deadbolt on the inside of the ground floor, exterior door, she discovered in the morning that the door was wide open, letting in moths and mosquitoes and...who knows what else? Her husband assured Jane that the previous night, the only water he ran in the sink was to brush his teeth.

That afternoon, after lunch, as they all walked down the village lane, her husband softy spoke to her, saying, "There's someone walking along with us. I can feel it. I don't know how to describe it, like a flat chill. It's a presence."

On the second night, as her husband contentedly snored, she heard heavy footsteps upstairs in the Tanyard. There were pounding sounds in the attic, and again, the sound of the door being opened to the children's room. She made a deal with the spirits, telepathically communicating to leave the kids alone, at least, and bother her if they had to bother someone. She said that was a big mistake... Lights shuddered, toilets self-flushed, and a mysterious and unwelcome heat invaded her body. The oppressive ghostly activity continued until five in the morning. Later that day, she found the Tanyard Journals on the shelf and read with some relief the comments written by other guests who had similar experiences with odd sounds and sights. That day, in the village, as she sat down to rest, the window behind her in the Meeting House seemed to come alive, buzzing, vibrating to its own rhythm. On the third night, Jane found herself awake and "alone" with the phenomena.

Jane, from Texas, writes:

A few years ago, I stayed with my family at the Tanyard House at the Shaker Village in Pleasant Hill. We experienced paranormal activity virtually nonstop. It was extremely disturbing. We fled after four days and did not complete our vacation. A lot of the experiences were relatively trivial, such as opening and closing doors, faucets turned off and on, flickering lights, footsteps, traveling cold spots, and so on. However, I could not sleep at night because "Polly" kept tormenting me. I heard a constant tapping in the walls and above our heads, and I felt extreme heat, as if I was going to burn to death.

Even my husband, an expert cynic and scientist, developed an odd relationship with Polly. He would play classical guitar for her, and she flicked the lights off and on if she preferred a certain piece. She especially liked Bach. I talked with some of the staff, and one man told me that Polly had been the "greeter" at the Village. She had also been the music teacher and had educated the young children. We have three young children. Someone else told me that an African-American family had lived for awhile in the Tanyard House. One of our children, adopted from Ethiopia, is black.

Neither my husband nor I were big believers in ghosts before the visit. Indeed, my husband was a determined non-believer. Those few days changed our minds forever. Worst of all, we were on vacation in Kentucky to escape something traumatic that had happened to someone we loved. It was a violent crime. Perhaps the ghost(s) were activated somehow by our grief. Who knows?

We did not feel that the ghost(s) were entirely benign. Indeed, I wish that Shakertown had informed us beforehand that they had ghosts. We never would have stayed there if we had known. One morning, I was in the Shakertown office, and two women were checking out from another room early. They said they were tired of the ghosts! I have written about the experience to "get it out of my system," so to speak. Just trying to heal, I suppose. We were at the village three years ago, and it has taken me all this time to get around to processing what happened. The combination of the crime and the paranormal stress was extremely difficult to bear, and it has taken me awhile to be strong enough to think about it with a little distance.

Postscript: Jane told me that her husband believed that the spirits traveled over 1,000 miles with her family, back to Texas. She had endured the ghostly manifestations for four days at Shakertown but drew the line at the thought of an unwanted ghost taking up residence in her own home. With her husband at work and kids off to school, she set up a circle of candles and lit them. With heartfelt words and intentions, Jane asserted that this spirit was not welcome. A half a dozen candles blew out with an odd snapping sound but she felt the spirit had left.

Tanyard and stone fence; view from field. *Photo by Thomas Freese.*

East Family Dwelling

Restless Rocking Chair

The largest building in the East Village is the East Family Dwelling. Built in 1817, this brick building has many rooms for overnight guests. During our Shaker singer retreats, I have stayed in various rooms throughout the East Family Dwelling, from the floor just above ground level overlooking the village lane, to the fourth floor rooms tucked up near the attic rooms. A former employee tells of a door that simply didn't want to stay locked! It was the bathroom door to a room on the top floor—the fourth floor. She also recalls a restless rocking chair on the third floor of the East Family Dwelling: "It would often be seen rocking back and forth."

Another village "hot spot" is the Trustee's Office. The Trustee's Office was built in 1839, and was the center of much activity, having served as the place for contact with the outside world. Here the society's trustees, those leaders who served as liaisons to the "world," lived and entertained visitors. Food and clothing were dispensed to the poor, and souls interested in becoming Shakers were counseled. The Trustee's Office is currently the site of much activity, containing a number of guest rooms and several very busy dining rooms. Graceful wooden staircases spiral up near the entrance to the dining area. We Shaker singers have often been given complimentary meals there during our retreats.

The Trustee's Office

Sounds—But No One There

Bruce Herring is the captain of the *Dixie Belle* riverboat, which is owned and operated by Shakertown. Bruce pilots the *Dixie Belle* on the Kentucky River, taking visitors on a short cruise from the Shaker landing. He is an entertaining and knowledgeable guide for his passengers. Bruce had previously worked at the front desk at Pleasant Hill, which used to be located in the Trustee's Office. He remembers a time about seven years ago when he was totally alone in that building. It was winter and there were no guests or employees about.

> I was working a shift from eight in the evening until eight in the morning. At that time, the village was actually closed to visitors. But on two separate occasions, I heard people walking around. I also heard a female voice singing. These sounds came from right above me, on the second floor. I walked out into the hallway... and I found no one there.

When I visited Shakertown in the summer of 1998, I wandered into the dining area of the Trustee's Office and asked the waiters and waitresses if they had any ghost stories to share. One employee remembered a young African-American lady who worked in the dining room. The woman saw a woman in white "floating" down the back stairs. The waitress dropped her serving tray and screamed, "There's someone out there! There's someone out there!"

It was reported that the young woman clocked out and promptly left for the day.

The Others in the Dining Room

Sarah Moran worked as a waitress in the dining room of the Trustee's Office for many years.

Recently, and many times previously, I've heard my name called. When I look around, nobody is there. That only happens on the porch. One time, after we had closed, I went into the east room of the Trustee's Office. There was nobody else in there. I had set up the tables with all their tableware and glasses and napkins. But later, when I went back into the east room, I noticed the silverware on the two larger tables had been messed up. A lot of times, things are just out of place. We put something somewhere and then it's seen halfway across the room.

Trustee's Office, Pleasant Hill. *Photo by Thomas Freese.*

Mandy Allen, a waitress in the dining room at the Trustee's Office, said:

> I've heard my name called quite a few times. I usually hear that on the porch. I've snuffed out a candle, only to later find that it's lit again.

Seth Brewer worked with Sarah and Mandy in the dining room. Seth said that, in the spring, a tray of juice glasses fell off a table, although there was nobody around the tray. He had heard of the same thing happening with a rack of plates.

A new waiter was working in the dining room. He said:

> I was training as a new employee. One night, we were moving chairs from the center room. We had to clear them for the morning buffet and put them in the front sitting room. My coworker was bringing them up to me and I was hanging them on the wall. As he was getting more chairs, I came in from the hallway and I saw the rocking chair start to move by itself. I dropped the chairs, turned around and ran out of the room! I pushed the other man all the way to the back of the building and told him what happened. I wouldn't go in there by myself at night for quite a while.

Figure from the Past

Eva P. Lay worked in the kitchen of the Trustee's Office dining room. One night, at about 9:30 in the evening, she left work and walked through the parking lot behind the Trustee's Office. Over in the adjacent parking lot to the west, she saw a man dressed in the old-fashioned clothes of the Shaker's time, including a hat. She noticed that he was not carrying a flashlight, but a *lantern*. Some of the folks in the kitchen later laughed at her and told her that it was probably one of the night security men. But the night security people don't dress up in Shaker attire and they carry flashlights, not "old-time" lanterns.

Perhaps the original Shaker Trustees still feel the need to supervise work being done in the building they constructed with their own hands. It is reported that when the men who were hired to work on the air conditioning and heating unit were in the attic crawl space, some of them have felt a tap on their shoulders. Many of the Shakertown employees have heard voices coming from "Whitehall." Whitehall is the back, third-floor hallway in the Trustee's Office building. It's called Whitehall because it is painted solid white. On the side of Room 311, there's a service door that leads to the air-conditioning units. Even when there is no one else in the building, sounds of people talking will filter down from that area.

East staircase of twin spiral staircases, second floor, Trustee's Office, Pleasant Hill. *Photo by Thomas Freese.*

Two employees, a married couple, were cleaning the cellar of the Trustee's Office one day. They were working in separate rooms when the man suddenly saw a young girl come in. She asked him a question before she went into the room where his wife was working. But later when asked, his wife said that she had seen no one come in.

Ghost Prefers Quiet

Maintenance worker Tucker said that he and his coworkers would work overnight, cleaning the ovens in the kitchen "pots and pans" room of the Trustee's Office. Tucker says:

I was down in the basement of that building earlier one night to work on a pipe. Before I went back upstairs to clean the ovens,

I stacked up some wooden crates to serve as a ladder to reach the pipe I was wrapping with new insulation. I returned to the kitchen and put a Janis Joplin tape on, as loud as it would go. Then I heard this racket. I had watched Joyce go out the door. I *know* I was the only one in the basement. Everybody had left.

When I went out to see what had caused the racket, I found everyone of those milk crates knocked down throughout that passageway. I was scared to death. I felt the hair stand up on my neck. I looked around to see if someone was in the building and I found no one. I even checked the time clock just to see if someone had come in and clocked out and left. I looked in both of the bathrooms... I was totally alone in there. Then I apologized to the spirits and turned off the music and went back to work.

Tucker acknowledges that many of the sounds the village buildings make are not the sounds of restless spirits:

Pipes will moan. I've heard that.

A former employee of Pleasant Hill worked as a night security person.

It was my first evening and I was out in the village doing the rotation, checking the buildings. I was in the Trustee's Office and I went up to check on one of the security clocks. When I went up the spiral stairs and reached the top floor, I felt something breathing down the back of my neck. But there wasn't anyone there. I don't know if it was first-night jitters, a ghost, or the boogie man.

Footsteps All Night

Cathy Bryant of Lebanon Junction, Kentucky, and her sister, Janet Robison, traveled to Shakertown in the early 1990s. Cathy said:

My husband and I had gone our first time and we enjoyed it so much. I wanted my sister to see Shakertown and to experience the food and atmosphere. We booked a night to stay together in a double room in the Trustee's Office on the third floor. Well, I had a great night. We went to bed and I really didn't notice anything unusual. The next morning I got up and said, "Janet, did you sleep well?"

Janet answered:

No, I didn't. Between your snoring and the footsteps in the hall, I didn't get any sleep at all.

Cathy asked:

What do you mean?

Janet replied:

I kept hearing footsteps. They would walk past our room... and stop. Finally, I got up the nerve to open the door and see. I thought someone was out there, prowling around. The next time I heard footsteps, I opened the door, and there was nobody there. I just know that there was a ghost out there last night!

The odd thing was that we were staying in the last room at the end of the hallway, and Janet heard the footsteps come down the hallway and go past our room. There was no place to go past our room at the end of the hall—right past us was the window.

Old Stone Shop and Creepy Feelings
Cathy continued with another story concerning the Old Stone Shop, located a short walk westward down the village lane.

My husband passed away almost three years ago, and I wanted to revisit Pleasant Hill, because there were some good memories there for my husband and me. Janet had just laughed at the experience of the footsteps, and we had a good time there. So my sister and I decided go back to Shakertown a couple of years later. I like to stay in the Trustee's Office, but we had called late for reservations. We were lucky to get in any building. They called us to let us know there was a cancellation. So we stayed in the Old Stone Shop on the top floor.

When we walked in that room we got the oddest feeling. We didn't want to spend the night there. But we had reservations. So I thought, this is crazy, we're just tired. We unpacked and went out for a walk and returned to our room. It still felt a bit strange.

We opened the little doors that went out to a crawl space under the eaves. There was one of those little doors by the bathroom and another door in our room. I felt a little creepy. We didn't sleep that well, although we didn't see or hear anything. It was just that *strange* feeling. I had never felt that before at Shakertown.

We Got Rattled

Pat DeChurch provided a story from her family's stay in the Trustee's Office building's room overnight.

In the early spring of 2001, my daughter, Lucynda Koesters, her two children, Nicholaus, age 10, and Andrea, age 6, and I visited Shakertown. It was a nice day. Being early in the year, it was not crowded and most of the shops were closed, but you could walk through every building. Everything was pleasant and peaceful until we went into an annex. There were three floors, all bedrooms used when the hotel was full. On the first floor was a sitting room. The second and third floors were all bedrooms.

Lucynda and Andrea wanted to walk up to the second and third floors. Nic and I waited in the sitting room. We were the only ones in the building. I remember how quiet it was. All of a sudden, Nic and I heard loud, loud, rattling.

We looked at each other and Nic said, "Mom must be trying to open a door."

We heard it again. The next thing we heard were Lucynda and Andrea racing down the stairs.

They burst into the sitting room exclaiming, "Did you hear that?"

I replied, "We did," and that we thought she was trying to open a door.

"Oh, no, we weren't doing a thing. The noise came from the third floor."

I certainly was curious and Nic wanted to check it out, too, so up we went. We were half way up the second flight of stairs when we heard the loud, loud rattling coming from a door on the third floor. That was enough for Nic. Down he went.

I stood looking at the door and I will forever be sorry I did not check to see if the door was locked or open. That was enough adventure for them and we left. The next building over, they were giving a demonstration on making brooms. We were standing to the left, where a window looked right into the building we had just left. The third floor was quite visible. When I looked at the windows the first time, the curtains of one room were closed. When I looked again, they were open.

What was all of this? Well, with all of the stories from Shakertown I believe this one can be added. Someone did not want us on the 3rd floor. We think it was unusual. It definitely left us rattled.

The Ministry's Workshop

Walking west from the Trustee's Office, one encounters a yellow, brightly painted wood building that was constructed in 1820. The Ministry's Workshop was sometimes where guests registered for overnight stays—the "front desk." This was where the ministers worked on Shaker crafts. After the initial restoration of Pleasant Hill, it housed guests in two rooms on the second floor. Like the other Shaker buildings, it has wooden, plank floors. The single-door entrance opens into a hallway with a staircase. The hallway is flanked by two small rooms.

Ministry's Workshop, Pleasant Hill. *Photo by Thomas Freese.*

The Ministry's Workshop was oftentimes the first contact visitors had with Shakertown, as the friendly staff located their reservations and provided a map and directions to get visitors to their accommodations. I often went directly from my drive of one to four hours to check in with the folks there and catch up a little on news and happenings in the Shaker village. I found the ladies who worked there very supportive of my intention to collect Shaker experiences.

Boxes Thrown About

Ruth Keller can share a few odd tales from her experience at the Ministry's Workshop. She is the front desk supervisor. Ruth has heard from upstairs the sounds of chairs being moved. Also, she was in the office with two men one time; they all heard sounds coming from the room above the front desk. At that time, there were boxes stacked up in that room. The night watchman didn't go up to have a look, so she grabbed the security guard and they climbed the stairs to investigate. They found that the boxes had been thrown about! Also, the door to the room which had been left open was slammed shut.

Ruth would often hear the sounds of someone walking upstairs. This happened even when the room was locked and no one was up there.

Sandy Inman, who does accounting at the Ministry's Workshop, notes that the rooms above the front desk had been guest rooms. She said that, sometimes, when the overnight guests had babies, the babies would wake up screaming for no apparent reason. The guests also reported seeing rocking chairs that would rock without any visible force.

One Pleasant Hill employee stationed in the Ministry's Workshop reports that her coin container top, which had been on the verge of breaking off, was found by her to have been mysteriously returned to better condition. This happened in her own money drawer to which only she has access and must be opened with two keys.

Michelle Dunn also works at the front desk in the Ministry's Workshop. She says:

> I would always grab the railing at about the third step from the top when I came down the stairs. It seemed to be an unusual habit of mine until I heard a story from a visiting psychic. The psychic had gotten the impression that a Shaker woman had fallen from that third step.

Michelle said the psychic told them the story she "saw."

> There had been a meeting upstairs of the elders and eldresses. During the meeting, the elders were not in agreement and a number of people had sided with one woman. An elder was upset about this. As they were going downstairs, the man may have pushed or accidentally stepped on the woman's dress. She fell down and was seriously hurt.

Michelle has heard a voice in the office of the Ministry's Workshop. She reports that when she heard the voice, she turned around to see who was talking to her.

She asked Chrissy, another worker, "Were you talking to me?"

Chrissy replied that she hadn't been talking at all. In addition, Michelle said that the television had been turned down, so the voices weren't from the television.

Shaker School Children

Michelle Dunn saw a group of adults and children going west on the village pike in March of 1999. She had arrived to work in the Ministry's Workshop and was headed to the front door when she saw this group. But the group of school children was clothed in Shaker attire and the girls had on dresses. Michelle smiled at the group and thought, *how quiet and orderly they are.*

It is indeed a rare sight to see a school tour at nine in the evening!

So You Wanted to See a Ghost?

One of the closest encounters in the Ministry's Workshop, and indeed in the accounts throughout the entire village, is told by a new Shakertown employee who started working at the front desk. Candy worked with Michelle and told her that she would very much like to see a ghost. The two walked through the village to see if they might spot a spirit gliding past on a warm spring night. On the following night, Candy and Michelle were busy working at the front desk. Candy had returned to the upstairs to put the receipts in her drawer when she rushed back downstairs.

Michelle noticed that she seemed upset enough to cry and asked her, "Candy, is something wrong?"

"There's a man upstairs," Candy said aloud, and one of the security guards who was there heard that and went upstairs to investigate. Bruce Herring was serving as a night guard that night and he stated that he certainly felt a presence there.

Michelle went to see if there were ghostly vibrations upstairs, but she hadn't gone halfway up the stairs when the hair on the back of her neck stood up and, she said, "My entire back feels like ice!"

Michelle and the other workers believe that the ghost had walked himself down those stairs.

Unexplained sights and sounds continued the next evening when a kitchen employee, who had heard pots and pans rattling in the kitchen basement, noticed that the Ministry's Workshop back door was wide open. This happened almost immediately after Michelle had closed and secured that same door. In addition, Candy was singled out again for a visit from the Shaker man. While Michelle was talking to someone at the back window, Candy came upon the same ghostly visitor at the front desk. He was taciturn and stared directly at her. She reports that he had a blue vest and a hat. His beard was long and his hair was brown. She will not forget his serious look.

When Candy called out, Michelle came, and by then, the Shaker specter had vanished.

Shaker Elders Stared at Me

Dolores Krier and her husband were overnight guests in the Ministry's Workshop thirty years ago. Dolores recalls that they had a choice of only two of the buildings at Pleasant Hill, since the restoration was recently undertaken. She explains that she and her husband slept on separate twin beds. The beds were very similar to the beds on which the Shakers had slept. They had a cross-woven support for mattresses filled with straw. Dolores says:

> We retired for the night. I woke up about three in the morning and I felt uncomfortable. I felt heaviness. I was lying flat on my back on the bed. When I opened my eyes I looked across the room, which wasn't very far, as the room was not big.
>
> I saw a series of faces appear. They showed themselves in black and white and they seemed to be male faces. Their expressions were very dour and unhappy. The faces came one after another. It was almost as if I was watching an old movie reel.
>
> The feeling that came over me was very strong. It felt like a pressure, an anguish or misery. And it was very, very heavy—I found it difficult to breathe. I felt so extremely uncomfortable. It was like everything within me was contracting. It was a feeling of pulling into myself.
>
> I turned on the light, and then the faces disappeared. But the *feeling* remained in the room. I woke my husband and I said, "We have to leave." It was pitch black, about three-thirty in the morning.
>
> My husband said, "It's the middle of the night!"
>
> I answered, "But I cannot stay here. I can't stay here a moment longer. I'm finding it difficult to breathe."
>
> We packed our bags, and we went next door to the Trustee's Office. We told the person at the front desk we were leaving. We checked out, and it wasn't until we were in our car and driving away from Shakertown that the feeling of pressure left me.
>
> Since that night, I have been back to Pleasant Hill for two or three visits in the last five years. I've been there as a day visitor. I have walked by the Ministry's Office where we stayed that night, but I had no strange feelings when I walked by there.
>
> I wonder if those vibrations, the energy of the Shakers, were more prevalent for my first visit compared to recent times, since we stayed overnight soon after the buildings were opened.

The Meeting House

Next to the Ministry's Workshop is the Meeting House. The Meeting House was the spiritual center of the village. It was where the Shakers had their dedicated worship. Although the Shakers considered their everyday tasks to be holy, the Meeting House was the place where they could support each other in the active and creative expression of their faith. In this building they would sing and dance and shake off their sins. The Meeting House was the site of many of their visions and was open to visitors. The Shakers looked to some of the inspired visitors as possible converts to their faith.

1820 Meeting House, Pleasant Hill. *Photo by Thomas Freese.*

The original Meeting House was located farther west along the village pike. It was close to where the present craft store stands. However, during the New Madrid earthquake of 1812, that building was substantially damaged. Plans were made and executed to construct the present meeting house. The solid construction of the Meeting House is proof of the Shaker's legacy of craftsmanship and evidence of their attitude: "Do your work as though you had a thousand years to live and as if you were to die tomorrow."

Despite the decline of the village and the disappearance of the mortal Shakers, the restored Meeting House has survived as a wonderful and enchanting place of worship and simplicity. The Meeting House had been adapted in the 1900s as a garage—you can still see oil stains on the floor—and as a Baptist church. It was built in 1820 and had upstairs apartments for the ministry. The Meeting House is entered through two doors, separate for the men and the women. No interior columns obstructed the view or provided a hindrance for dancing and whirling. There are matching, small windows on both the men's and the women's sides where the spiritual leadership observed the worshippers from the stairwells and checked for potential converts.

The Meeting House is a large structure, measuring sixty by forty-four feet. I heard a National Public Radio program with Joel Cohen from the Boston Camerata. He often visited the Shakers at Sabbathday Lake Maine. He described a Shaker Meeting House as an instrument in itself. He noted that the Shakers built the underlying floor joists farther apart than usual so that, in addition to the percussive sound of the stomp on floorboards, there would be a satisfying bounce back.

I think the Shaker singers and I, and likely many of the Pleasant Hill employees, viewed the Meeting House as the spiritual center of Shakertown. I have been built up with emotion while stomping, dancing, and singing on the same floorboards that the Shakers shook up long ago. For speaking, and particularly singing, the acoustics are bright and bouncy, and songs carry even outside to the village lane. I have spent many meditative moments, in morning, afternoon, or evening sitting on a bench in the Meeting House, wondering if I might connect with the spirit of the Shakers. I can anytime easily close my eyes and visualize the Meeting House interior and see faces of visitors as they listen and imagine what Shaker life was truly like.

Mysterious Singing

A visitor can find daily music and dance programs in the Meeting House. In addition, there are talks on Shaker spirituality and candlelight performances held there. Before the current Administration Building was constructed, Pleasant Hill's offices were located upstairs. Shakertown employee Ruth Keller would sometimes have to go up into those upstairs offices to turn off computer stations that had been left on. She would unlock the empty building and, two or three times, she heard singing on the first floor.

First-floor interior of the Meeting House, Pleasant Hill. *Photo by Thomas Freese.*

Many employees have heard singing in the empty Meeting House. Karen Preston, a former employee of Pleasant Hill, was making copies in the upstairs of the Meeting House one winter evening when the building was locked. Karen heard singing downstairs.

It was a female voice... sort of doing a scale of notes. I called Ralph to come help check it out and to meet me downstairs. At first, I thought that perhaps a radio had been left on. But we found that all the offices were closed and there were no radios still on.

Another Pleasant Hill singer recently heard a ghostly voice coming from the Meeting House. James Lochridge said:

44

A practice had been scheduled for the Pleasant Hill Singers for a Friday evening at 6:30, but was cancelled without me knowing about it. I arrived at the Administration Building but no one was there, so I started walking to the Meeting House, the other place we usually practice, but on the way didn't see anyone else in the group, so I was starting to wonder if practice had been cancelled. As I approached the Meeting House I heard distant singing, so I was glad that I'd found where we were practicing. As I neared the east side door, I clearly heard the voice of a woman singing a pentatonic scale, which the Shakers used in many of their songs, and continuing on to the front of the building past this door, the voice faded. On reaching the front, I found both doors locked and nothing but silence from inside. I might have second-guessed what I heard when it seemed at a distance, but there's no question that I heard distinctly the woman's voice as I passed the side door, the pentatonic scale unmistakable. Sadly, there was no one else around at the time to confirm what I had heard.

Shaking Wall Sconce

A female employee of Shakertown who worked in accounting tells a story that perhaps reminds us of why the Shakers got their name.

We were in the Meeting House upstairs. This was some years ago, when the offices were there. I was talking with a coworker about some of the weird things that happen at Pleasant Hill, when we noticed that the light on the wall was shaking. It was a wall sconce, and there was no reason for it to shake like that. There was nothing else in the office moving. There had been no earth tremors that day.

A former employee who worked with public relations at Pleasant Hill was also an interpreter in the Meeting House. She noted an experience that happened about fifteen years ago.

I had finished up a session. I'd been interpreting for a group. One woman stayed after all the other group had left. She was a charismatic who was visiting from Atlanta. She was wearing regular attire, blue jeans, and a tee-shirt.

She set her four-year-old daughter on a bench, and came up to me and asked if she could "twirl." I saw no harm in that, and the woman proceeded to spin herself, dancing, in the middle of the Meeting House. The woman spun for at least fifteen minutes without stopping. She spun with her arms out and hands upward.

Then she suddenly stopped, without being dizzy at all. She picked up her child, thanked me and left.

Even if we do not see or hear the Shaker spirits, perhaps their invisible presence nonetheless pushes us to take up their typical worship dancing by proxy. It seems this visiting lady was connected to the joyful and consuming sort of spiritual body actions as also often led the Shakers.

White Shadow Figures

Andrea Yussman, Louisville, says:

This ... is rather more of a little shadow sighting. It happened very quickly, but I knew what it was because I have experienced this many times before at other places, like in my own home.

I visited Shakertown six years ago. I was with several ladies who I taught with at Thomas Jefferson Middle School. All I remember is we'd just finished lunch and we were touring around the place. We took a boat ride on the Kentucky River. Before we left Shakertown, we visited this area that looked like a church or meeting place. I felt like there were spirits on the grounds because I remember seeing white shadow figures. They moved quickly especially in the area of the Meeting House.

I remember seeing the white shadows streak by me very quickly as the woman in front of the church was talking to the audience. I never said anything to anybody, not even the people I was with. I knew what I saw and this was long before I even read Thomas Freese's [earlier] book on Shakertown ghosts. At that point, I never even questioned the place being haunted by ghostly spirits. Sometimes it's better to keep quiet and not alarm people about sightings. However, there are a lot of non-believers and they all think you're crazy when you mention it. This was not a bad thing, but you just question what you saw or didn't want to acknowledge what you saw.

Even though it was a beautiful sunny day, the brightness of the white shadows far outweighed the sunshine. Along with my unique score of souvenirs—like jewelry and hand-crafted baskets which I bought at Shakertown—I also have the memory of an incredible encounter on a carefree afternoon.

Angel Shout Calls Shakers to Meeting

Bill Bright, a former Pleasant Hill employee, tells of an amazing experience.

It was in the winter of 1996, and Dixie and I were working in the village. She noticed that the candles from a candlelight performance were still in the windows of the Meeting House. Dixie decided that they needed to be put away, so we stopped in there. I helped gather up the candles and Dixie went to put them in the closet.

Since I was a bit bored, I walked over to a spot between the two front doors to sing a little. I was next to a gap in the wall benches, facing the back wall. I started to sing sets of three, descending notes—triads. Since I had spent plenty of time in high school band, I figured that it'd be a neat exercise to try the acoustics in the large room of the Meeting House.

Three windows shine on hardwood floors, Meeting House.
Photo by Thomas Freese.

As I was singing, something appeared in the middle of the benches to my right, on the sister's side. For lack of a better explanation, it looked like a human form, very similar to the special effect done on *Star Trek* when they beam up somebody. It seemed to rise up from the floor to my height. At that point, the hair on the right side of my body stood on end, while the left side was not affected. I immediately got cold chills, like I had just walked into a meat locker. I just wanted to get out of there. I left the building immediately, quickly enough to make Dixie come out after me.

She asked me, "What's wrong?"

I told her what had happened and she suggested that I talk to Randy Folger, the music director. When I saw Randy, I told him about the experience and he simply asked me if I knew what I had been doing. At that point, I had no idea. Then Randy asked me to sing as I had been singing in the Meeting House. After I sang for him, Randy explained to me that I had unwittingly been singing the "Angel Shout." The Angel Shout was a set of notes that were sung like: "Lo... lo... lo..." and were sung in descending thirds. The Angel Shout was supposed to call the Shakers to meeting.

Today I have no reservations about going into the Meeting House, but I will not try my experiment again!

Strange Goings On

Randy Folger relates:

We had reason to believe that there was something odd in the Meeting House. And so that was the main place that we wanted to check out and see what it was like. To tell you the truth, there was supposed to be something bad in there, according to this woman who couldn't come in one time.

I was getting ready to do a performance in the Meeting House, and Beverly was at the door. A woman was getting ready to come in, and she started trembling, and she broke into tears.

She said, "I can't come into this room!"

And Beverly said, "Why, what's wrong?"

And the woman said, "Something terrible happened here. Somebody was killed in this room. There's bad here, I can't come in this room."

And she couldn't—she couldn't set foot over the doorstep.

Also, about six months later, a friend of mine came down from Lexington, a woman I used to work for. She has a cottage at the lake, and she stopped by to visit.

I said, "Well, let's go over to Shakertown. I'll show you where I sing."

In those days, the Meeting House wasn't restored the way it is now—where the two side windows are now was blocked in and there were two little closets. And so I took her in there. When we walked in the Meeting House room, we were close to the northeast corner where my little office was. All of a sudden she started trembling!

She said, "Oh, my God! Somebody was killed here!"

I thought back to the time with Beverly and the woman who wouldn't come in.

I said, "What do you mean?"

She said, "Somebody was shaken to death, here! There was a young girl, and for some reason or another, they thought that she was possessed of spirits, and they shook her to death. They killed this girl, right here on this spot!"

I was astonished.

But she said, "No, there's something wrong—there was a window here. This can't be right, because there was a window where this wall is..."

And I opened my closet, and there was the window! It had been sealed up, because of the closet.

"That's it!"

She said, "I see it... The time of the year was the fall. This girl was murdered, basically. And there are about four or five Shakers standing here. One woman was speaking in tongues, while this man was shaking her to death."

I took her down to the office, and we were flipping old photographs. She even picked the girl out of the photographs.

She said, "This is the girl... and here's the guy that did it. And here's the woman who was speaking in tongues."

So, we *knew* that there was something about the Meeting House!

Shaker Spirit

In 2006, I received an e-mail from somebody who read my first book, *Shaker Ghost Stories*. Bryan Collins was very interested in both the Shakers and in the stories of the Shaker spirits. Bryan was already a talented craftsman, making beautiful nesting Shaker swallowtail joint wooden boxes, when he and I exchanged emails about his interest in joining the Pleasant Hill Singers. Bryan enjoyed performing with the Singers for a time, and his interest in the Shakers was rewarded with a Shaker experience. Bryan said:

On Tuesday June 5th, 2006 I took a vacation day to deliver my Shaker oval boxes to the Kentucky Craft Market Program's jury session in Frankfort. The process took less time than I had anticipated, and, as a result, I had the greater part of the day to spend as I wished.

I hadn't originally planned to go to Pleasant Hill on this day, but with this new free time, I figured I could take Highway 127 from Frankfort to Harrodsburg and then on to Shaker Village. I rehearsed a song in anticipation of joining the Pleasant Hill Singers. I felt it would be a good idea to try to alleviate some of my performance anxiety by spending time in the 1820 Meeting House. When I pulled into the parking lot at Shaker Village, I called the Trustee's Dining Room and made reservations for lunch. I asked for a late seating to allow myself plenty of time to walk around the village, shop the craft store, and spend some quiet time in the Meeting House.

I obtained my Friends of Pleasant Hill pass at the Craft Store. The attendant asked if I was there recently during the week and I told her I was not. She said, due to low attendance on some weekdays, several of the buildings weren't open. Buildings they kept open accepted visitors on a limited basis. I made my way down the 1837 Turnpike toward the Meeting House. The village was mostly deserted with the exception of an occasional employee.

I sat down on the first row of benches in the Meeting House and thought *what a beautiful day this was turning out to be*. Each visit I make to Pleasant Hill is special to me. I feel fortunate to be able to experience this treasure of Kentucky. I sat quietly for fifteen minutes or so. When it became obvious there weren't visitors walking the village and employees were few and far between, I thought it wouldn't hurt to softly sing a few notes of the song I had chosen to sing for the music director. I began by humming a few bars of *The Humble Heart*. Although I never burst fully into song I was able to sing enough to know I would be just fine when it came time to sing for the director.

Sitting on the front row of benches allowed me to see out the door of the Meeting House and directly across the turnpike into the entry hallway of the Centre Family dwelling. Although both front doors were open, there were low gate-like barriers blocking entry to the Centre Family dwelling. Each barrier held a sign stating the next hour visitors could tour the building. During peak days visitors are able to enter most any building in the village and wander at will. There are docents who give brief talks on each building's use and Shaker life. However, that day the village staff and activities were unusually limited.

Centre Family Dwelling, Pleasant Hill. *Courtesy of the Library of Congress.*

During the last of my moments spent in the Meeting House. I glanced across the turnpike and I saw a woman sitting in the hallway of the Centre Family dwelling. I saw her profile as she faced the opposite wall of the entry hall. The profile view didn't allow me to see her face because it was hidden by her Shaker bonnet. She had on the traditional Shaker blue dress with a white collar kerchief across her shoulders which came to a point in the front. She sat very stoic. Her hands were folded in her lap. I did not give this lady much thought at all because, in my mind, she was just one of the employees. The only thing I distinctly remember thinking at the time was *oh, I hope that is my friend Georgie; I'll go over and talk with her*.

My performance jitters being soothed, I got up from the bench, walked down the steps of the Meeting House, crossed the turnpike and started through the gate. I looked up a couple of times on my way there to see if the lady would turn toward me so I could tell if it was Georgie or not. The amount of time it took me to go from the bench in the Meeting House to the gate at the Centre Family dwelling could not have been more than fifteen to twenty seconds because it is a short distance. The couple of times I glanced up while walking toward the lady, I found she had not moved. When I was sure of my footing on the first of the steps leading up to the Centre Family dwelling front doors I looked up again. I was close enough now that if it was Georgie or even another docent, then good manners dictated a greeting. I looked into the front hallway and the lady was gone. It was as though someone threw cold water on me. I continued on up the steps half frightened and half knowing there was some sort of explanation. A person could not go anywhere that quickly.

So where was she? Surely she had stood up and walked to the center of the entry hall and I just couldn't see her from the steps. I continued on up the steps. I approached the front door, stopped at the barrier and stuck my head in the entry way. Complete silence; nobody anywhere.

I turned and started back down the steps. My legs were weak and I felt somewhat shaken. My analytical mind was still trying to process what just transpired. This was my first experience where I actually saw something without an explanation. I walked down to the Trustees Dining Room and had lunch. My stomach was full of butterflies and I didn't feel like eating. I sat throughout lunch staring out the window just dumbfounded. I recall during lunch, as I recovered from the initial shock, a feeling of thankfulness coming over me for having this experience.

I read Thomas Freese's book, *Shaker Ghost Stories*, prior to my experience. Admittedly, I may have unconsciously made myself open to the possibility of seeing a Shaker spirit. I haven't added to the details nor taken from them. I have related this experience to my sister, my best friend, and Thomas Freese. I did not go to Pleasant Hill that day ghost hunting. I think that is *the* most surprising part for me—how totally off guard I found myself. Bewildered would have been a good way to describe myself several days afterward.

Outside the Meeting House, on the village road, there have been a few sightings. The village pike was actually US Highway 68 until the creators of the restored Shakertown wisely diverted the highway farther south. It is now a peaceful village lane lined by trees. Visitors find Pleasant Hill employees demonstrating crafts in the shade of the trees. Soldiers from the Civil War re-enacting camps, occurring every other year, march down the pike, much like the traveling armies of the Union and Confederate forces did in the nineteenth century. Visitors ride horse-drawn wagons on their Shakertown tour. It is common to see the Pleasant Hill employees, dressed in Shaker attire, walking to work or back from lunch.

When I visit Pleasant Hill, I love to walk down the village lane. From the walking road that leads from the parking lot, past the gift shop, I quickly get to the heart of the village. A glance east or westward down the village pike gives me a rapid assessment of how many visitors are about that day and what kind of demonstrations are happening. I've enjoyed the peaceful pike in all kinds of weather, and it's pleasant to stroll down the lane and look at the marvelous Shaker buildings, or to view the lane from inside one of the wavy glass antique windows.

Randy Folger, who was the music director for ten years, was everyone's dear friend and he inspired many a visitor with his sweet voice and kind eyes. Randy provided me with a number of the Shaker ghost stories and he was interested in the unusual happenings. Since I began gathering the Shaker ghost stories, Randy, and a number of other Pleasant Hill interpreters, have passed on.

Shakers Shout at 3 a.m.

Randy Folger told of an interesting event that occurred during the 1996 Civil War reenactment. He said that many of men who were portraying the soldiers knew very little about the Shakers and their type of worship. They had placed an overnight sentry at the corner of the Centre Family Dwelling, across from the Meeting House. Susan Lyons Hughes, the Education Specialist, checked on them the next day.

Randy said, "These guys were terrified!"

The sentries asked:

What the heck was going on last night? At three in the morning, we heard the most awful racket coming from the Meeting House. We heard people clapping their hands and singing. They were stomping and shouting too!

Randy said that they were very serious about the truth of their experience. "They discovered how the Shakers worshipped."

The former waiter, who told of the rocking chair that moved, heard from some of the Civil War re-enactors, too. He stated that two soldiers told him that they were in front of the Meeting House one night. They saw two figures approaching from the west end of the pike. The figures were carrying lanterns and were dressed in Shaker clothes. But when they got closer to the re-enactors, they disappeared. The waiter said:

> Another man was walking down the street in front of the Trustee's Office. He saw someone go by him who was dressed in Shaker attire. He figured it was Randy Folger, and he wondered why Randy didn't greet him. As he thought that, the employee turned around to discover that the figure had vanished.

A former Pleasant Hill housekeeper told of a couple of guests who were walking down the village pike one evening. They reported that a man, dressed in Shaker garb, was walking toward them. The couple was walking from the Trustee's Office toward the West Family Dwelling. As they approached the man and prepared to speak... the man simply disappeared! The couple reported being firm disbelievers in ghosts *before* this incident.

One overnight guest to Pleasant Hill saw a disappearing figure walk across the village pike. When I was visiting Pleasant Hill to perform a Christmas program with the singers, Bob Woodruff was excited to tell me his story. He had made many trips to Shakertown, and had heard of encounters with the Shaker ghosts, but hadn't really ever expected that he would have one himself.

Shakertown interpreters walk westward on village lane, Pleasant Hill. *Photo by Thomas Freese.*

Shaker Woman Disappears

Bob said:

On the evening of December 11th, 1998, I was walking west on the village road. There was an overcast sky and no wind. It seemed like rain was about to fall and it was a little cold. There was no one else about and it was *very* quiet.

As I came up to the Trustee's Office building, by the little turnaround drive, I saw a woman cross the village road farther down. She walked from the Meeting House to the Centre Family Dwelling. She looked like a Shaker. She had a long, blue dress with a white apron and a white bonnet. I even noticed the bonnet details. The bonnet was of solid material with a wide brim across the front and sides. It completely covered her hair in back. The wide side brim shielded her face from my view. The white bonnet and apron stood out in the dim light.

She passed right next to the lamp post, going from the eastern gate outside the Meeting House to the matching gate directly across the lane in front of the Centre Family Dwelling. It seemed that her hands were in her pockets. Since I had just an hour previously arrived from California, I was tired and thought no more that she must have been a docent working there. I looked away from her for a few moments. When I looked back she was gone.

I assumed that she had gone into the building, or perhaps around the other side of the Centre Family Dwelling. I was curious. When I reached the building, I circled completely around it and listened for her. I looked for her white clothing in the darkness but the Centre Family Dwelling was dark and the doors were locked and there was no one to be found.

It was only then that I realized what had happened, and I felt very fortunate. While I have had more dramatic "encounters" at my home, this was my first experience at Shakertown.

Centre Family Dwelling

The very large Centre Family Dwelling dominates the central village at Pleasant Hill. It stands across the village road from the Meeting House. The two buildings provide a historical focal point and visitors are often found in either building or standing on the pike between the two. The Centre Family Dwelling took ten years to complete in 1834, and is an architectural marvel, inside and out. Large white limestone blocks provide sturdy walls. The inside is spacious and inspiring with its tall ceilings and broad hallway. Just inside the entrance, historical interpreters greet the visitors. They patiently explain building features, exhibits and Shaker customs. Some of the rooms display Shaker industries, such as seed packaging, cider-making, and weaving. There are other rooms with separate brethren's and sisters' beds, some with small linen bags strung on the bedposts. The bags have herbs to repel insects.

The Centre Family Dwelling has three floors exhibiting exquisite Shaker craftsmanship in architectural detail and exhibits. A large bell on the roof of the ell is rung by the interpreters to call visitors to the Meeting House for music programs.

When I sang at Shakertown, I usually had the opportunity to go into the Centre Family Dwelling. I wandered throughout the building and tried to locate one of my favorite cats who was often found inside the Centre Family Dwelling or outside on the limestone steps. I felt like my visit was complete if I had a chance to pet Mischief, the tortoise shell tabby cat.

Centre Family Dwelling. *Photo by Thomas Freese.*

Former feline resident of Shakertown, Mischief. *Photo by Thomas Freese.*

Shaker Spirit Sings

Carol Zahn, an interpreter who worked in the Centre Family Dwelling, said that she and the other interpreters have heard singing there.

> A number of times, when we're closing up the Centre Family Dwelling at 5:30 or 6, we have heard the soft sound of an older woman singing. This has come from the upstairs meeting room. I am not surprised that there are Shaker spirits in residence here. The Shakers believed their spirits stayed here until Judgment Day.

Carol is a dear friend and Shaker singer who has now passed on. She loved to hear about the Shaker ghost stories, and she and her daughter had a few of their own stories from their home.

Sarah Thomas, who worked as an interpreter at the Centre Family Dwelling, said:

> I've gotten a weird feeling when I'm upstairs in the infirmary exhibit. And an odd thing happened once when I was cleaning out spider webs in the loom room. I had cleaned out the spider webs in all the other rooms without any problem. But when I came back into the loom room after about five minutes, there was a whole new batch of spider webs there.

Interpreter Mrs. Mary Lee Woford had guided visitors through the Centre Family Dwelling for many years. She had been a Shakertown employee for twenty-four years. Mrs. Woford would often be seen standing near the entranceway to the interpreter's tiny office/closet as she waited for the next group of inquiring souls to enter the Centre Family Dwelling. A number of her fellow interpreters noticed something interesting on the one-year anniversary of her passing away, in 1998. The lovely and strong scent of lilacs could be smelled right at her favorite spot.

Gill Lay worked in maintenance at Shakertown for eighteen years. He had an odd encounter in the Centre Family Dwelling when he was working there one winter evening around 5:30. It was dark and he had set up three or four lamps on the first floor in order to be able to see to mop the entire floor. He recalls that it took about an hour to mop the floor prior to waxing it the following day.

> I had of course locked the outside door of the Centre Family Dwelling. I finished mopping and went upstairs to use the third-floor bathroom. When I was up there, I heard footsteps downstairs. I hollered, "What are you doing down there?"
>
> Nobody answered. Nobody was down there or in the building with me. I asked the other night worker and he hadn't been to or in the Centre Family Dwelling at all.

Blast of Cold Air

Beverly Rogers has worked at Shakertown for over a decade. She can be found in the Centre Family Dwelling with other experienced and talented interpreters.

We were having a performance for the Friends of Pleasant Hill Forum. We always had it on the second floor of the Centre Family Dwelling in the meeting room.

The Meeting House is across the village pike from the Centre Family Dwelling and the meeting *room* is upstairs in the Centre Family Dwelling.

One of our administration employees had been in the brothers' room, the first room on the right, when you enter the building.

She came out, scared to death, and said, "I'll not come back in this building at night. '"

I asked her, "What happened?"

She said, "I had a cold breeze blow up my dress!"

Farm Deacon's Shop

The Farm Deacon's Shop is located close to the Centre Family Dwelling and it was the original Centre Family Dwelling. It is the oldest permanent structure at Pleasant Hill and was built in 1809. It is a two-story stone structure and is a short walk west from the Centre Family Dwelling. There are a few stories of ghosts from folks who have worked in the Farm Deacon's Shop. Some of those stories will come later in this book. Following is one story related by interpreter Carol Zahn.

A Chill and a Bad Feeling

I've felt or seen a number of strange things at the Farm Deacon's Shop. The Shakers had used the building for a number of purposes: family dwelling, tavern, shop, and residence for the farm deacons. Some of us interpreters working there have heard footsteps upstairs, and the creaking sounds of boards being walked on, up and down the staircase.

Some of the interpreters have smelled lilacs there. Also, some workers have felt an oppressive male presence in the Farm Deacon's Shop. Oftentimes, we've noticed strange things happening when the village was almost vacant, during the time when the majority of tourists were gone.

I was alone one time, in the Farm Deacon's Shop, when I got the feeling that someone was watching me. I sensed that someone was outside, near the window, next to where I was sitting. I felt the hair stand up on the back of my neck, and I had a cold feeling come into my body. I heard the sound of walking in the cellar below. I felt that someone was *in* the cellar, looking up at me through the cracks in the floorboards.

I was so scared that I couldn't talk. I couldn't wait until the twenty minutes were over when I could close up and go. I couldn't get out of there fast enough. I had the overwhelming feeling that there was something there I didn't want to see!

Farm Deacon's Shop, Pleasant Hill. *Photo by Thomas Freese.*

The Carpenter's Shop

Near the intersection of the east/west village pike and the north/south village lane is the Carpenter's Shop. The Carpenter's Shop is located diagonally across the intersection from the Farm Deacon's Shop. The Carpenter's Shop is a brick building constructed in 1815. It was used as a blacksmith and wagon shop until 1843. It was rebuilt in 1870 for the manufacture of brooms. The Carpenter's Shop is currently the Pleasant Hill Craft Store. The Craft Store is a well-frequented building for many a visitor at Pleasant Hill. Each time I went to a Shaker singing performance, I liked to take a fellow singer and we'd walk down the village lane or the parallel orchard road to the Craft Store. It was warm in winter and cool in summer. And we easily spent our one-hour breaks between performances there. There are books, candles, woodwork, musical tapes, and Shaker-reproduction swallowtail boxes. I both window shopped at the Craft Store and parted with real money, when I felt flush with cash.

Rose Sorrell worked in the gift shop, which was first housed in the Farm Deacon's Shop. After she'd worked there for two years, the gift shop was moved to its present location in the Carpenter's Shop.

A Gentle Voice
Rose related:

> Early on, in the new building, I noticed a man's voice. It was a gentle voice. I only seemed to notice it when I was getting ready to lock up and leave. I'd say that I heard that voice about once a month, and only when I was right at the door. I didn't tell anyone else about the voice because I thought I was the only one who heard it.
>
> Well, one time I was again at the door, but with a coworker. We both heard the voice simultaneously! We looked at each other, and I asked her, "Did you hear that voice?"
> She said, "Yes!"

That's when they *both* admitted to hearing the voice. The other worker said that she wasn't sure if it was a voice or a noise, and if a voice, whether it was telling them to get out or to stay.

On another occasion Rose and Amy Inman McGinnis, and some other workers, were in the Craft Store downstairs, in the break room. They were at the kitchen table when Amy said she heard the sound of running water. She heard this sound *over* the noise of the television that was turned on. They looked and found that the water was running full stream. They turned off the water, but several minutes later, the running water was again heard. They never had any other problems with that water faucet, before or since that time.

Crafts store, historic Carpenter's Shop, Pleasant Hill. *Photo by Thomas Freese.*

Hear the Angels Singing
Paschal Baute says:

It happened about ten years ago now. My wife and I were visiting Shakertown with friends. We had left the restaurant and headed toward the Gift Shop to the right. I decided I would rest in the shade on an August day with a breeze of September in the air. There was a bench (no longer there) and a tree. I would wait while my friends visited the Gift Shop.

Suddenly, to my right a few feet away, appeared a little girl; her age I would guess was about five. She had dark hair and dark eyes.

She looked at me and announced, "I can walk in a circle!"

Surprised, I decided to play a teasing game with her.

"On, no," I replied, "You can't walk in a *circle.*

"Yes I can!" she replied.

"No, you are too little!" I continued.

"But I can," she insisted.

"No, you can't," I said. "You are not old enough."

"Yes I can," she insisted.

Finally, I said, "Show me."

To my surprise once more, she raised herself to her full height, looked me in the eye and said: "Why should I?"

Oh God, I said to myself; *I am in the presence of the Eternal Feminine.* After my teasing her, here she was, teasing me back. How utterly delightful! After a moment I said, "Please?"

She proceeded to walk in a circle. By this time we had been together for several minutes. I wondered where her parents were— possibly looking out a window of the restaurant we were next to. But I saw no sign of them. With nothing else to do and this precious little girl willing to entertain me, I decided to continue the playful teasing.

"I bet you can't walk in a square."

"Yes I can."

"No, you can't."

"Yes I can."

We went through the whole rigmarole again.

When finally, I said, "Show me."

She said "Why should I?"

I said, "Please."

So she showed me.

Next, we went to a triangle with the whole similar teasing dialogue once more. Again, after my teasing her, I had to beg her to show me. My geometry was exhausted.

As we finished our third round of play, my wife and friends came out of the Gift Shop and indicated to me they were ready to continue their walk to see the Village.

"I have to go now," I said to my little mistress, reluctantly, as I had enjoyed the experience at least as much as she, maybe more.

"No!" she shouted.

And then I repeated, "NO, you can't leave!"

We had both become entranced with the little game we were playing. What was I to do? I had guests. Where were the parents of this precious little girl? In hindsight, I wish I had offered to take her to them or to meet them. Feeling pulled from both sides, I thought of a way to leave her with something else to do with her imagination.

"Do you believe in angels?" I asked my little angel.

"Yes," she responded, without delay.

"Then come here and sit on this bench and I will tell you a secret. If you sit here and sit very quietly you can hear the angels singing."

By the way, angels have been a part of my own belief system since Catholic grade school. She readily complied, sat on the bench and closed her eyes. Reluctantly, I turned to join my friends. Turning back to glance over my shoulder, I saw her sitting quietly on the bench with her eyes closed, in some listening repose. I never saw her again.

I was so impressed with this experience I talked about it and even wrote about it. I cannot now find that writing. I have a vague memory that her name was "Ariel," but I do not remember her telling me that. I will wager that she did hear the angels singing because she remained very still as I looked over my shoulder walking with my friends out of her sight.

I have wondered since what she remembered of our playful exchange, that one day when an aging balding man was entertained by a little angel. At the end, I thought to introduce her to the angels, not realizing I had just perhaps been visited by one. My wife told me later that she would not have believed my story, except that she saw the little girl. For me, it was a visitation, unexpected, serendipitously, a mysterious exchange on a late summer day with an old man willing to be present to the moment of whatever with a like-minded child.

To this day, I wonder where her parents were, or if she had any parents. I wish I had taken her to her parents and praised her smartness. I am sure she was and is gifted wherever she is. I can easily imagine her delighting many others with her "tricks." That visitation to me may help explain why I am in love with my encore career of Spellbinder storytelling in Lexington, now in my 5th year. I love being with children and telling stories.

Paschal Baute is a Spellbinder storyteller with the Lexington, Kentucky, chapter of Spellbinders. He is completing a book, *Storytelling: Mystery, Power and Genius, or How Storytelling Nurtures the Human Spirit.* His website is www. paschalbaute.com.

Old Stone Shop

Continuing with our ghost tour, imagine again walking west and across the village pike to the next Shaker building. The Old Stone Shop, made in 1811, was a West Family dwelling and later became the village medical office. There are now rooms for overnight guests. If you stay in one particular upstairs room, you can find an undated poem written in pencil on the stucco wall. The poem is in room 174 and is located near a window. The restorers kindly left a frame around the writing, leaving the poem intact with new stucco all around it. One could imagine a woman, having given up the fullness of marriage, writing this heartfelt remembrance:

Dost ever thou think
O Darling fair loved one
of the first time we stood linked
in each other's embrace
Dost think as thou goest on the way
of that time when my heart
was so full with love overflowing
That I spoke not but kissed thee
and sent thee away

As I read this intimate note, I tried to imagine what life was like for young women in the nineteenth century, and how their choices might be limited to being homemakers. But suppose your husband was killed in the War Between the States, and your land and home were legally given to another male relative or in-law. Sacrificing love and property to join the Shakers might be a wise choice. The Shakers gave their children a fine education, and hard work was done by all but the very rich anyway. But it did tug at my heart to read these lines of lost love.

Some folks, in a sort of Shakertown urban legend, have connected this poem with a Shaker journal mention of a young Shaker woman who hung herself. Although the event must be true as reported by the Shakers, according to Larry Currie, the building in which that tragic event happened no longer exists. Yet visitors sometimes take away the story and mistakenly believe that the woman committed suicide in one of the remaining structures. Here below is a curious tale.

Sad Scene
Dave Shelton relates:

In May 2001, my wife and I went to visit her cousin, Robin, in Kentucky. She took us to visit Shakertown at Pleasant Hill. She had briefed me in general as to the nature of the Shakers and mentioned that the Shakers had interactions with the "other world." But she didn't tell any specific stories.

We spent the night in one of the Shaker buildings to the left and far back from the main building. That night, after I was sleeping, I had a vision of walking up to the attic. There I saw a shadow curled up on the floor. It felt swamped in sadness and anger. To me, the shadow seemed to be replaying a hanging scene which I assumed had taken place in the attic. In the vision, I helped to guide her out and she went away in the sky.

On the next morning we had a fabulous breakfast and toured the village some more. When we went to check out, the computer had us owing nothing for the rooms or breakfast! They tried to figure out what happened, but told us we owed them nothing. We tried to pay them for the services we received, but they refused us.

Apologized to the Spirits

Susan Hughes stayed in the Old Stone Shop one night. She had been working at Shakertown during the weekend of a funeral reenactment. It was late at night and she was tired. As she went into the Old Stone Shop to prepare for the night, she announced out loud to the spirits that she wanted to sleep. She told the spirits that she wasn't in the mood for any of their visits.

She tried to sleep, but she kept feeling like a feather was being pulled across her nose. After about an hour or so, she turned on the light.

She said aloud, "I'm sorry, I didn't mean to offend you." Then she found that she went to sleep without further incident.

I found one humorous ghost story from the Old Ministry's Shop. This is a wood building that is a little northeast of the Old Stone Shop. It was built about 1812 and had a variety of uses, including service as a school house at one time.

Old Stone Shop, Pleasant Hill. *Photo by Thomas Freese.*

Old Ministry's Shop

Door Kept Opening

One of the Confederate re-enactors, Stephen Bowling, was giving tours of the Civil War encampment. I chatted with the re-enactors about their camping weekend, and I eventually got around to asking them about Shaker ghosts. I figured that they were rugged guys who probably looked at life realistically, and that they likely didn't believe in ghosts. But the re-enactors immediately spoke up about something that had happened that weekend. They had been in the Old Ministry's Shop. They had closed the back door, but found that it kept popping open.

The men would yell, "Come on in!" Then they'd get up and shut the door. This happened four times. Perhaps the ghost of a Shaker schoolboy was finally able to play some pranks without facing the teacher's punishment.

Across a wide lawn space where the Civil War re-enactors camp from the Old Ministry's Shop, is the West Family Sister's Shop. This is red brick building, two stories tall. The West Family Sister's Shop was constructed thirty-two years after the Old Ministry's Shop was built. The Shaker women, as productive and industrious as the Shaker brethren, pressed and packaged medicinal herbs. They also made carpeting and corn shuck mattresses.

West Family Sister's Shop

Just *Who* Was up Last Night?

Guests from Louisville, Mary Hand and her husband stayed in the West Family Sister's Shop in the mid-1990s. Mary thought they came in the fall, as she remembered it being cool and they used the fireplace.

My husband had a lumpy bed and we got him on a different bed in an adjacent room. I kept hearing footsteps throughout the night. They seemed to be going to the bathroom. I thought that my husband must have had diarrhea. I felt sorry for him because I heard the footsteps going all night.

About three in the morning, I again awoke to hear footsteps going to the bathroom. I decided to check on him and make sure that he was all right. I waited and waited outside the closed bathroom door. After a long time, I knocked and then looked into the bathroom to discover that nobody was there. I looked down the hallway and I could see my husband sleeping in his bed.

I was sleepy and confused and I once again went back to sleep... still hearing footsteps. This time they were coming up the steps. I was a bit concerned, and I looked out to check for an intruder. Once again, there was no one there. I fell asleep and dreamt that I was telling my friends that I had spent the night at Shakertown, with ghosts.

I asked my husband in the morning if he had been up to use the bathroom. He said that he had slept soundly. He hadn't used the bathroom all night!

Rose Sorrell remembers some customers who came into the craft shop where she worked. They had stayed overnight in the West Family Sister's Shop. The man said that he was awakened from his sleep by hands that were shaking him. He said that when he looked about, he saw that his wife was fast asleep.

A few other buildings close to the West Family Sister's Shop which also carry some good ghost tales are the West Family Wash House and the West Family Dwelling.

The West Family Wash House sits almost next to the West Family Sister's Shop, separated only by a small building, the Preserve Shop. The Wash House was built in 1842.

West Family Sister's Shop, Pleasant Hill. *Photo by Thomas Freese.*

West Family Wash House

Vanishing Figure

Bruce Herring, the riverboat captain, relates a story told to him by Marty Gray. He said that Marty was checking up on things in the West village. He'd decided to walk instead of drive the night security truck. Looking up into the windows of the West Family Wash House, he saw someone inside who was standing by one of the windows. He went into the Wash House and looked all around, but discovered no one inside.

One of the Civil War re-enactors previously worked during the night security shift at Pleasant Hill.

I would get eerie feelings, and the hair on the back of my neck would stand up. I remember getting those feelings in the West Family Wash House and in the West Family Dwelling when I was upstairs. I felt like I was being watched. I get that same feeling when I go into my grandmother's house, which is supposed to be haunted.

West Family Wash House, Pleasant Hill. *Photo by Thomas Freese.*

West Family Dwelling

The next and last building in the tour of village haunts is the West Family Dwelling. The West Family Dwelling was constructed in 1821. The older Shakers lived there and were assigned duties requiring less strenuous labor. It's a large structure with a brick front facing the village pike. The cool basement cellar served as a morgue in the Shaker's time.

The West Family Dwelling is close to the other West village buildings. They're grouped at the west end of the turnpike and are the last historic buildings one sees on the way to the graveyard. The Shaker singers sometime have stayed overnight in the West Family Dwelling during retreats. And we often eat our lunch before a warm weather performance, down in the basement summer kitchen.

West Family Dwelling, Shakertown at Pleasant Hill. *Photo by Thomas Freese.*

Spirit Fascinated with Lights

Stephen Bowling and his fellow re-enactors from the 4th Kentucky Volunteer Infantry had a Shaker experience there. Stephen said:

> Two years ago, we held our Civil War encampment. We were driven into the West Family Dwelling to spend the night because of rain. We were upstairs and in the back room. Well, the men couldn't find a switch to turn off the lights.

The light bulbs are in reproduction wooden wall sconces.

> The guys unscrewed all the bulbs so we'd be able to sleep better without the lights being on. One light bulb came on, so they unscrewed it again. Then *two* bulbs came on and they got up and unscrewed those again. They actually then took out those two bulbs, completely removing them from their sockets. Then another one came on! In the course of an hour, four bulbs came on, just as quickly as they could get them unscrewed. And the door to the restroom swung open as they unscrewed the last light bulb.

There are rooms for overnight lodging in the West Family Dwelling. In addition, there are larger meeting rooms, and in the basement cellar, a lovely summer/winter kitchen.

Marty Gray and another maintenance worker were called over to the West Family Dwelling. A guest in a room on the first floor had reported hearing the sound of scratching on the door. Arrangements were made for the guest to switch to another room. Then Marty and his coworker spent the night in the guest's room, waiting to see if perhaps a raccoon had gotten into the building.

After a while, they heard the scratching sounds, too. When they turned on the lights and looked at the door, they were surprised to find scratch marks on the *inside* of the door!

One employee started out working for Shakertown in the summer kitchen as a waitress. It is a long dining area, with wooden octagonal supporting pillars. There are large whitewashed stones that make up its walls. A waiter reported that the new waitress was working in the north room of the summer kitchen.

> She was serving vegetables and passing by a table of two patrons, when she felt somebody jab an elbow into her side. She almost dropped the vegetables. She thought that it was Michelle or one of the other girls who hit her by accident. She went back into the kitchen and asked her fellow workers, "Which one of you all bumped into me? You almost made me spill a bowlful on those people."

And they all said, "We've been back here!" The waitress couldn't explain what happened.

Leona Inman, who works at the front desk, tells of housekeeping workers who were at the West Family Dwelling. They had cleaned a room and then locked it. Later, they heard the sound of furniture being moved in the same room. When they unlocked the room to have a look, they found that all the furniture had been moved to the middle of the room.

Ghostly Presence

A man from Buckhorn, Kentucky, stayed in the West Family Dwelling.

It was October of 1993; my wife and I and our two-and-a-half-year-old daughter had gone to Shakertown to meet with my brother in law and his wife. They had gotten married there about seven months before and they had wanted to come back. We stayed in a house that had four separate living areas, each one consisting of a bedroom with a sitting parlor, and a main parlor downstairs. As we were checking in we got word from them that they were going to be late. They were supposed to be there at four in the afternoon. We got there at five. They had told us they'd be there about eight. About seven o'clock we were sitting down in the parlor waiting for them to drive up.

We heard a door open upstairs. We heard footsteps along the upstairs hall. Then we heard the footsteps coming downstairs, through the hallway and going out the front door. But the door never opened and there was no one on the stairs.

My wife and I were thinking, *we're going to get out of here now.* Our daughter made the comment, "Well it's okay, he just wants us to know that he's going to take care of us." And so we stayed there and in about twenty minutes Tom and Andrea came. We haven't yet told this story to anyone because we didn't think anyone would believe us, but that's what happened!

Shaker Room Service

Another incident which occurred in the West Family Dwelling was told to me by the employees of Shakertown. An overnight guest reported that a woman dressed as a Shaker knocked on her door at five in the morning. This out-of-state guest had stayed at Shakertown many times. She works for a hospice and was visiting Pleasant Hill with her mother. The Shaker-dressed female used a key to enter the room after knocking, and she carried a stack of fresh towels. The guest expressed surprise at receiving this housekeeping call so early, and the Shaker woman reportedly replied that it was a courtesy extended to them. The guest then asked that she at least please be quiet so as to not awaken her mother.

In the morning, the woman noticed that the towel which she had used to wipe off her makeup was either gone or had indeed been cleaned by the Shaker woman. Later that morning, the guest inquired about the unusual timing of her "room service." She was accurately informed that the housekeeping staff wears a simple service uniform which does not resemble the period Shaker clothing. In addition, housekeepers report for duty at an hour more convenient for most mortals.

Finally, the female guest stated that the Shaker ghost had been running the clothes washer and dryer, located below her guest room, all night.

It seems that the Shaker spirits are as dedicated to helpful service in their new lives as they were when they assisted each other and "the world" as mortals.

West Lot Dwelling

Two stories from two other sites are fascinating to hear. The West Lot Dwelling is west of the village proper and takes a short drive of one and one-half miles to reach. The drive is beautiful and takes the visitor over Shawnee Run Creek. The West Lot Dwelling is an impressive limestone building which stands on high ground and overlooks rolling hills. This building was occupied by those persons who were not yet fully Shakers. They had not signed a covenant of full commitment to the Society of Believers. Shakertown employee Dave Brown relates a puzzling experience from the West Lot Dwelling.

West Lot Dwelling, Pleasant Hill. *Photo by Thomas Freese.*

I worked at Pleasant Hill for five years and I'm currently the front desk supervisor. My first job, though, was in meeting services. We would set up and take down the meeting rooms. The West Lot Dwelling is the primary conference area for the village.

Who is Walking Upstairs?

We had two meetings going on down at the West Lot. One night, while working late after a particular group had left, I was cleaning the upstairs room while waiting for the downstairs group to finish. It was probably eight-thirty or nine o'clock on a winter evening, so it was fully dark. I had cleaned the upstairs room and I had some electronic equipment that was still out, so I dead bolted the two interior doors from the inside and went out the side door and locked it behind me with my key.

By this time the other group had left, so I went downstairs and started clearing the coffee pots and cleaning up. That's when I heard the footsteps. I was in the basement and heard the sound of footsteps walking from one end to the other on the first floor. I didn't really give it too much thought at the time, because we have people walking around these buildings all the time. But I got to thinking, *maybe I better go up and check.* When I went up I found the two interior doors were still bolted from the inside and the upstairs door that I had exited was still locked. I thought that maybe one of the maintenance guys had been over to check in with me. I called the front desk to ask if there was anyone staying in the building that night. They told me that no one was staying there. Then I talked to the maintenance man, who was on duty, and he said, "No, I wasn't down there; I had no reason to be there."

It struck me as weird because the sounds of the footsteps were very distinct. I heard them not once, but walking back and forth. There are all sorts of funny things out here. You'll catch things out of the corner of your eye. It's not anything that you can put a finger on, but you'll see little glimpses of things. A couple of times I've had an eerie feeling, like someone was looking at me. The hair on the back of my neck will stand up and I'll just know that a ghost is there. I recognize that feeling from a haunted apartment my ex-wife and I had in California.

Mysterious Shaker Wood Spirits
Lois Madden, from New Richmond, Ohio, says:

I've often pondered the happenings of that late day June hike at Pleasant Hill, and just thinking about it awakens memories that I still find chilling! It proved an unforgettable day…and night.

That June day at Pleasant Hill dawned beautiful and quiet. I just love the way the day awakens there. It's so peaceful. I was excited because the Pleasant Hill Singers, along with the rest of the interpretive staff, were presenting "The Day of Releasement" program. It's a fun-filled afternoon of song and dance, period games, and picnicking on the grounds. I was especially looking forward to hooking up with my dear friend, D. R., who was driving down from Cincinnati to participate in the day's events and stay overnight. She and I don't get to spend quality time with one another as often as we'd like. This day was one we were both looking forward to sharing.

The day was perfect for the event, but as can happen in mid-June, the day quickly turned quite hot. Although I was pretty tired by day's end, I was too keyed up to just run into town and have supper. D. R. and I concurred that a walk on one of the newly opened hiking trails would be just what we needed to wind down. After consulting with one of the staff, we headed over to the West Lot area to pick up a short trail. As we climbed the gate to access the trailhead, a bunch of cows, grazing in the adjacent field, greeted us with their mooing.

So began what I've dubbed our "Shakertown Blair Witch Experience." Not long into our hike, I ventured off the trail to rock hunt in a creek bed. I can't bypass any opportunity to rock hunt. I found one that caught my eye and decided to "collect it." I always say a prayer of thanks when gifting myself from Mother Nature's bounty and that day was no exception. The exception was that I didn't have the tobacco I usually offer up as a gift of thanks in exchange for what I'm taking with me. I didn't think the Wood Spirits would mind.

I rejoined D. R. on the trail and we went on our merry way. It's my practice to notice interesting nature art as I walk in the woods. This practice also serves as a tool to identify visual landmarks in case I get turned around along the way. The Wood Spirits didn't disappoint. I spied this incredible exposed root on the hiking trail that looked like a smoker's pipe. My husband is a pipe smoker, so it jumped out at me. D. R. didn't quite see the pipe in that root but I did and thought it was amazing!

The day was fast waning. It was getting cooler, darker in the dense woods, and a gentle rain had started falling. We were both getting tired, wet, and lank. We decided to reverse our steps and head back to the West Lot and head to Harrodsburg to eat at a favorite Mexican restaurant. The Wood Spirits had other plans in store for us.

We journeyed on and on and on. It soon became obvious that we weren't getting anywhere. I kept stepping over the exposed pipe root, but we just couldn't seem to get beyond that point on the trail. We kept walking but we weren't making any progress. The woods had changed, not just the texture of the day, but the energy surrounding us. The air felt ominous and charged somehow. I can't really explain it with words. It was an oppressive feeling.

My level of concern was growing by leaps and bounds. D. R. was becoming frantic. We hadn't come prepared to get stuck in those woods. It was supposed to be a quick, easy, relaxing hike. Hence, we had no cell phone, not that it would have worked in the woods, and no compass. We were dressed in light clothing, due to the heat of the day, so we weren't prepared to spend a night out in those woods in the rain. Gratefully, we did have bottled water. I knew we weren't lost because we were still on that marked trail. We just weren't making any progress reversing our steps. No one knew we were out there hiking and no one would miss us.

It was time to stop and regroup. D. R. and I talked through different scenarios but nothing we came up with offered us much comfort. At that point, I felt like the Wood Spirits were playing with us and I was getting frustrated with their games. My inner voice strongly suggested I return the rock I'd picked up earlier. I often ignore that little voice, but not this time. That rock went back in the creek with no hesitation. I then took a few deep, cleansing breaths, centered myself and offered up a prayer for guidance and deliverance. It wasn't long before we heard rustling in the woods to our left.

I have to admit we were both out of sorts with our hiking predicament, so the noise from the woods was a bit hair raising! I felt like we were being watched. As I peered deeper into the woods, I noticed a deer standing there watching us. I felt this incredible calm overtake me and I knew this beautiful deer was the answer to my prayer. We stood there watching each other for a few minutes when the deer started slowly walking in the direction we were headed and we slowly followed her. She'd stop, wait for us, and move on. That deer stayed within our line of vision, guiding us until I started hearing cows mooing. Once I heard those cows I knew we'd made it back to West Lot safely. That deer stopped, looked at me, then turned around and disappeared into the woods. I said a prayer of thanks as we climbed that gate and walked back to the parking lot.

We were wet, exhausted, exhilarated and looked like two wild women. We headed to Harrodsburg and had that Mexican meal we'd been looking forward to all day. I'll never forget the way the locals looked at us when we entered that restaurant—we were a sight!

Little did we know that the Shakertown spirits weren't quite finished with us! After our meal, we returned to our room in the West Family Sister's Shop. We showered, settled in, and talked until the wee hours of the morning about our experience in the woods. We finally fell asleep sometime before the light of day dawned. Sometime before daylight, D. R. woke me from a very deep sleep as she was scared. She was convinced there was someone in the room with us. Not long after that, I heard the sound of the Shaker rocker moving. I glanced over to where the rocker was sitting and saw that it was indeed moving. It was rocking as if a person was sitting in it, rocking it back and forth. That was it for my dear friend—she'd had enough. She got up, dressed, gathered her belongings and hit the road. I don't think she'll ever return to Pleasant Hill. I wasn't nearly as concerned about our visiting Sister. All I wanted to do was roll over and go back to sleep!

The North Lot

Shaker Resident
David Toczko tells us:

It was May 25, 2007. I, along with two fellow photographers, was on assignment to photograph Shaker Village of Pleasant Hill. Our assignment was to document the Village as well as cover the Chamber Music Festival of the Bluegrass, a two-day event being held at the Village. With a total of three days of photography ahead of us, we opted to stay at the Village.

Because of the large crowds, we were unable to get rooms on the Village proper, but rather at one of the Gathering Orders referred to as the North Lot. Although very close to the property, the North Lot is about a mile and a half drive from the property. When we arrived at the Village, we met with the Marketing Director and went straight to work. It was not until late evening that we went to the North Lot for the night.

North Lot House, Pleasant Hill. *Photo by David Toczko.*

As usual, we were reviewing the photographs taken that day. The three of us were sitting around the kitchen table sharing with each other what we felt were our better shots. I was sitting at the head of the table. Tom was across from me at the other end of the table, while JD sat to my right, his back to what we would later discover was a bathroom. After about an hour of review, I heard a door latch lift and the door to the bathroom behind JD swung open. All three of us froze at the table, looking at each other as if to say, "Did you see that?" At first, none of us spoke, looking at each other and shooting glances at the bathroom door.

JD broke the silence when he looked at me and asked, "What just happened?"

"I don't know," I replied and got up to have a look.

The door had one of those "Shaker latches" on it rather than a door knob. It is a hinged device that slipped behind a metal bar to secure it closed. As we were all sitting at the table, I didn't think the door could have shaken loose from us moving around. I closed the door and secured the latch. I lifted the latch to see just how much effort was required to open it. It was a rather snug fit and I didn't think it could have worked loose on its own. To further add to the mystery, when I lifted the latch, the door did not swing open on its own, but rather stayed close to the jamb. I had to pull the door open to access the bathroom. Someone or something had to have opened it.

While JD and I remained open minded, Tom discounted the event and went about trying to duplicate it. He stomped the floor... The door remained closed. Thinking JD had bumped against it with his chair (something both JD and I KNOW didn't happen) he pushed against the door trying to dislodge it from its latch...nothing. Finally, he tried to discount it by saying we were tired and imagined it, but all three of us had seen it at the same time. Was it fatigue or group hallucination? I think not.

Knowing we had an early morning ahead of us, we decided to turn in for the night. Tom and JD headed upstairs with me at the rear to turn off the lights. As I started up the stairs, I paused, turning around and said "goodnight" to whoever was with us. The rest of our stay was uneventful. I did not experience any other strange happenings and if my fellow photographers did, they did not share them with me.

The Graveyard

No account of a haunted village would be complete without a tale from the graveyard! The Shakers' cemetery is located one-fourth mile west, along the village turnpike. It is a peaceful site on a small knoll with tall evergreens and cedar trees. As it has been restored, there is now a neat, white wooden plank fence surrounding it. When I visited Shakertown, coming for the singing performances, I had walked to the graveyard and stood outside the wooden fence. I wondered if the Shaker spirits were present there, but I really didn't feel anything. Also, I didn't hear any stories during 1998 and 1999 when I gathered the majority of the ghost stories. I was a little disappointed that such an exciting village for spirit activity had no ghost story from the graveyard. But eventually, I was given the name of a man who, it was suggested, had an intriguing tale to relate. I am grateful that he shared it with me. And, years later, after my first book about Shaker ghosts and a Singers performance, a woman told me her story from the graveyard. Here they both are…

Shush!

She mentioned that she and her husband decided, during the visit at Shakertown, to follow the map and walk down the lane to the cemetery. They enjoyed the outside sunshine and chatted out loud. As they approached the white wooden fence, they drifted apart by some ten yards, still talking in loud voices to make comments back and forth. She heard a voice say, "Shush!" She turned to her husband, got his attention and asked him, "Did you just 'shush' me?!" He replied, "No I did not 'shush' you." She reported that, after that happened, their auditory tones were a bit more subdued as they walked around the Shaker graveyard.

Self-Risen Tombstone

Many decades ago, before the restoration of Pleasant Hill, the graveyard was a wild and wonderful place for young boys to explore. Twin brothers who lived near Shakertown set out with one of their buddies on a summer day, looking for a bit of adventure. The twins were twelve years old and their companion was ten years old. Their friend seemed to be one of those boys whose adventures often got him into trouble. They walked over the "kissing bridge" and past the ruins of the Shaker grist mill. On other days, they might have played in that creek or crawled up the mill's dried-out aqueduct.

Shaker cemetery at Pleasant Hill. *Photo by Thomas Freese.*

The trio went east along the old pike, traveling the same historic road on which stagecoaches had driven. They headed over to a favorite pond and checked out frogs and fishes. But the pond wasn't too exciting. They'd fished there for a number of years. So they wandered over to the rough place that had once been the Shaker graveyard. The smaller and nameless markers had long been grown over. Only a few and taller headstones were visible, and three boys with blue jeans had to scuffle past thorny locust and scrub cedar to find those gravestones. It took them a while to work their way through a small jungle of vines and honeysuckle. The youths crawled into a small clearing by a tree and found a few headstones waiting for their inspection. The Shakers were a modest people and most of their grave markers were only a foot tall, perhaps rough hewn from sandstone or field limestone. Many of those short stones had disappeared beneath a century of dust and natural debris. But the later Shakers had relaxed some of the Order's strict rules, permitting a person to have a musical instrument, a print on the wall as decoration, or...a standard height tombstone, completely carved with name, dates, and a saying. One taller gravestone they found was most likely one of the Pennebaker tombstones. The Pennebakers were two brothers who lived in Pleasant Hill. One became a doctor. Kids are curious to read headstone carvings, wondering about the name of the deceased, when they were born, and when they died. But moss and lichen had built up over the tombstone.

One of the twins figured out that they could scoop up some dirt and use it to try and rub off the thick moss from the marble. They worked on the headstone, removing some moss and trying to read letters and numbers that would tell the story of a deceased Shaker. After they had satisfied their curiosity, the younger lad suddenly decided to push the gravestone over. It fell with a *thud* into the weeds. The twins sensed that even boyish pranks and juvenile experimenting has its limits, and they worked to right the heavy stone while the prankster watched. After some trying, the third boy felt guilty and he lent his help to the efforts to lift the stone. As hard as they tried, though, the three boys simply could not bring the Shaker monument to its original spot. Six foot of marble could weigh 500 pounds.

The boys walked about twenty feet over to the only other visible headstone still standing, to have a look at it. It tilted slightly and had less moss on it. As they were examining the second stone, one of the twins felt a rush of cold air on his cheek. He looked back at the first gravestone. It had come back up, by itself, to its original position! The boys all stared at the self-risen marble monument for a moment in shock and disbelief. They then escaped from the brambles at a speed greater than their entrance, scared to death of the power of the unknown.

It took the twins thirty years to return to look for the self-rising tombstone. One of the twins, a man mature in his years, told me that the third boy can be found in the state penitentiary. The twins <u>did</u> locate that same pair of gravestones.

People wonder what the character of the Shaker spirits are like. I tell them that they are a lot like the way they were when living their mortal life. The Shakers, when alive, were singing, dancing, working, and believed in being helpful to others. Perhaps a guardian Shaker spirit was simply offering kind help to three boys…who couldn't fix their mistake.

Pennebaker tombstone amidst trees, Shakertown graveyard. *Photo by Thomas Freese.*

Some Interpreter Stories

I made wonderful new friends when I joined the Shaker singers. Three of those new friends were Dixie, Beverly, and Randy. All of them had been working at Shakertown for many years and each one seemed very dedicated to serving the public while dressed as Shakers. Beverly and Dixie were interpreters and Randy was the musical director. The Pleasant Hill interpreters are tireless workers who, for minimum pay, patiently explain Shaker lore to hundreds and thousands of visitors. They wear reproduction, Shaker clothing. They bake bread and pies in the Shaker, brick-lined ovens. They sing and dance and speak of Shaker beliefs. They explain exhibits and clarify the Shaker world view, usually while standing on tired feet. They represent not only Shakertown, but also the Shakers themselves. Some visitors believe that the interpreters are current-day Shakers. Many a time, when we finished our Shaker singing program, and formed a receiving line outside the Meeting House, folks were convinced that we were Shakers. The interpreters are the next best thing to traveling back in time for those who come and want to know more about these dedicated and spiritual folk.

Randy, Beverly, and Dixie were all Pleasant Hill Singers, and employees. And being around the village so much, they had a number of Shaker ghost stories to share. I interviewed Beverly and Dixie at Shakertown. I visited Randy Folger at his nearby home and recorded our interview on cassette, though some of his best stories came when we were later walking with no tape recorder. Here are the stories of who they are and what they saw and heard.

Dixie Huffman,
Beverly Rogers,
and Randy Folger,
left to right.
*Photo by Thomas
Freese.*

Dixie Huffman

I was born in a house that is on land once owned by the Shakers, just down the road a little. I taught school for thirty-one years, second through fourth grade, in Mercer County. At that time, I was teaching in the largest elementary school in the state under one roof, with over 1,100 students. I did enjoy the teaching. A few years ago, the frame building that had been next to my family home was torn down. That was a public school named Shakertown Elementary, and my mother had taught school there. When I was two, we moved over to a tenant building on what was the Shaker's West lot area. At the age of six, we moved to Harrodsburg. It had been too far for me to walk to school. The Woodard family had bought the West Lot land in 1917, and kept it until the mid-eighties, when it was sold to the Pleasant Hill Corporation.

I was raised in the Southern Baptist Church. I've belonged to the same church since I was nine years old. I have a brother who lives in Tennessee, and I have a sister, Betty Jo, who also works at Shakertown as an interpreter. I have three daughters, six grandchildren, and three great-grandchildren. They occasionally like to come to Shakertown.

I started at Pleasant Hill in 1971, working weekends and summer months. Then I retired from teaching in 1979 and became a full-time employee. It's been twenty-nine years. Back then, the season started in the middle of March and went to the last of November. I didn't work as many days in the winter. Sometimes, I would come for the winter weekends. I really enjoy being here. I enjoy the people that we see. I like the atmosphere. Whenever you come into a Shaker village you find a sense of peace and quiet and well-being. You leave the entire outside world behind.

Dixie Huffman and Pleasant Hill singer Mary Brinkman, left to right. *Photo by Thomas Freese.*

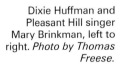

I liked Dixie because she had an even-keeled temperament; she seemed very straightforward, yet at the same time quite kind. Dixie was one of the local Mercer County inhabitants who'd been there a long time. I bet she had many more stories not even in the ghost category.

Spirits Provide Sweet Scent

Dixie said that she has smelled the strong, sweet scent of lilacs under the stairway in the cellar of the Centre Family Dwelling. She says that she and Beverly were both walking down the turnpike one day, when they simultaneously looked at each other, smelling a strong lavender scent, and then the perfume was gone.

Shaker woman in rocking chair. *Courtesy of the Library of Congress.*

Dixie reports that spirit-people have been seen sitting at the loom upstairs. As Dixie headed out of the Centre Family Dwelling at closing time one day, she looked up and saw a woman in a green dress who was looking down the stairs.

Dixie describes her sister, Betty Jo Peavler, as a "no nonsense" person. She said that, one day, Betty Jo left the Centre Family Dwelling, and walked across the village road to do a tour in the Meeting House. She unlocked a side door, and then went over to one of the front doors to open it for the public. The door was unlocked but she could not pull it open. There was no reason for it not to open. Betty Jo asked a man on the other side of the door, outside, to pull hard to open the door. He did and he went flying backwards. The man wondered what was wrong with Betty Jo.

One Halloween, Dixie experienced some unusual events. She was in the Centre Family Dwelling when she went upstairs to use the bathroom. She heard the toilet flushing, and she thought that there might be someone in the adjoining restroom. But as she looked at the toilet right in front of her she saw that an invisible someone had pulled the toilet handle.

Dixie reported that a couple, who had recently stayed in the East Family Brethren's Shop on the second floor, told her that they heard strange sounds from the attic. It sounded like someone turning over in or moving a bed. The "bedsprings" were creaking; and it went on for some time.

On Halloween, Dixie and Ella were working as interpreters in the Farm Deacon's Shop. The wooden barrier gate inside the shop started rattling, and wouldn't stop. This went on all day. Dixie and Ella checked the furnace to see if it was causing the rattling. They tried bouncing on the wooden floorboards, but they couldn't make the gate rattle. She says that the gate never rattled again.

I was finishing the research for the first *Shaker Ghosts* book and went around the village to obtain signed releases for the use of people's names in the book. During that trip I received yet more stories. Dixie related another fascinating tale.

Brilliant Light

Dixie relates:

One night, there was going to be a program of Shaker music in the Meeting House presented by the Pleasant Hill Singers. This was before I joined the Singers. I liked to come over and hear them on Saturday nights. They were singing for a group from the Friends of Pleasant Hill. I was standing in front of the Meeting House as I was waiting for the program to start.

I looked over to the Centre Family Dwelling and I saw the most brilliant light in the transom and around the door. I thought, *what in the world is causing that?* I stood there and looked at it for a while...

and it went off. It just stopped. And I didn't think about telling anyone else until we got through singing. Then I told Randy Folger, the music director, about what I had seen.

We decided that we'd better go over and check the doors and the windows. This was before we had the alarm system. The light looked like it might be coming from the cellar. It was a bright, reddish-orange. We came over and checked all the windows and all the doors, but nothing was open. Then we went over to the front desk and I asked the girl who was working there, "Has anybody been over to the Centre Family Dwelling?" She said, "No, no one's been there. No one has checked out the key." I told them what had happened and they didn't know what to make of it, either. No one had been in the Centre Family Dwelling. No one could have gotten in there, and I'm the only one who saw the light. Although there had been other people standing there, I had never thought to ask them if they saw it, too. It was the strangest looking bright red-orange light, maybe like a glow. I never figured out where it came from. And I've stood over there at night and many other times, and that's the only time I saw that light.

Beverly Rogers

I've been in Kentucky since 1973. I am originally from New Jersey. When we moved to Florida, I did not work, because we had children who were growing up. When my youngest child went to school, I started working at Pleasant Hill. That's when I really became involved with the Shakers and their history. I've always been an interpreter. I volunteered some time during the winters, and sometimes, I did journal research. This is my thirteenth year as an employee of Shakertown. I sing with the Pleasant Hill Singers and I love it! I live nearby, in Harrodsburg.

Beverly Rogers, (with Dixie, left and Randy on right).
Photo by Thomas Freese.

Strange Sounds

I was in the Farm Deacon's Shop. It was late afternoon, in October. There was a thunderstorm. It was about five in the afternoon and it was very dark, very dreary in the building. I heard something upstairs fall. At that time, you could go through the doors and go upstairs. I went upstairs and went through the guest rooms to see what had fallen. But there was nothing that could have fallen. There was nothing I found on the floor. So I went back downstairs and sat on the chair... I heard it again! I thought *maybe there's a loose shutter or something on the third floor.* So I went up to the second floor and halfway up to the third floor and I thought *what in the world am I doing up here?* I ran down the steps, three at a time. I *still* didn't see anything that had fallen down. I got down to the first floor door, shut it and locked it. And then I caught my breath, panting, after rushing downstairs. I felt like I was blocking "it" out, whatever had dropped this thing up there.

When I went home, my son said, "Mom, if it was a ghost, he could have gone right through you." And I said, "No, they would not have done that. Because then they would have had *my* spirit, living in that building with the Shaker spirit, and they *never* would have put up with that!"

That really did scare me and I called Dixie. I guess I was scared, also, because it was so dark, and there was thunder outside. Whatever it was that fell, I have never found it.

What attracted me about Beverly was her spunk, and I also got the feeling that here was someone who would stand by you, thick and thin. I felt a bit insecure when I joined the Shaker singers, not the least reason being that I didn't know how to read music. I also didn't belong to the Mercer County locals, nor was I even a Kentucky native. But interacting with Beverly, I felt that it really didn't matter. We were there to have fun and learn, and she was always happy to see me!

For many years, Beverly worked weekends in the Meeting House, where she sat in a little room adjacent to the large meeting room, waiting for the visitors. As she sat there with the door partially open, sometimes she would hear singing. She'd look out into the Meeting House and no one would be there. One day, Dixie came in and asked her about the music director, Randy Folger.

"Where's Randy?"

"Well," Beverly said, "he left a while ago."

Dixie replied, "He did not, because I heard him singing in here."

Unexplained Breeze

Beverly relates another story.

About two years ago, a woman and her eight-year-old child were touring the Centre Family Dwelling. The lady and her little boy came downstairs and said that they had been in the loom room. She asked us if we had seen or heard anything there before. Then she described how they had seen the apron on the bonnet moving back and forth. The bonnet apron was the fabric attached on back to keep the sun off a person's neck.

"But," the visitor said, "there was no breeze in that room."

Of course, there couldn't have possibly been a breeze in the room. We don't keep those windows open because we aren't up there very much. And we are supposed to keep the windows down because the windows have ultraviolet blocking.

What Happened to the Birds?

We've seen several things in that room before. I feel it's one of the rooms that are very active.

As part of her duties, Beverly would often unlock and prepare the Meeting House prior to a special performance.

I saw two birds at the window inside the Meeting House. The Meeting House had been locked and all the windows were shut. The birds were chimney swifts, and are found at the windows every once in a while. Their wings make them look like bats. And I thought, *how am I going to get them out?* Since the Meeting House has really tall ceilings, it's difficult to get the birds out. Also, if they've been in the chimney, they'll make a black mark if they brush up against the ceiling. So I walked over to the Sister's door to open it. When I turned around, the birds were gone! I hollered at Dixie, from the doorway: "Dixie, get over here!" I walked down to the Administration Building. I was scared to death. I think it scared me because I saw something *physical*, and then it was gone and I couldn't find it. I didn't have any explanation for it. *Where the heck did the birds go?* I didn't go by myself into the Meeting House for a while after that.

Vibrating Window

Besides the disappearing birds in the Meeting House, Beverly noticed that a window in the Meeting House displayed an unusual trait.

When the administration office was in the upstairs of the Meeting House, I would go upstairs to go to the bathroom. The whole building was air conditioned then, and everything was closed. The window that was in the stairway on the Sister's side would *shake* every once in a while—not vibrate once or twice—but go "*Hmmmmmmmm!*" One night, I had to go somewhere. I went upstairs to change from my Shaker clothes into my "worldly" clothes. When I came down those stairs, I thought the window was going to fly out of its frame. I looked at the window, and said, "I'll put the clothes back on tomorrow, I'm going out." As soon as I had said that it stopped, just *instantly*. And, I got to the point that when I came into the Meeting House on weekends, when I was alone, I would say as I went up the stairs, "It's just me. Don't worry about it, it's just me."

Someone's Behind Me

I asked Beverly, "What are your religious beliefs?" She said:

I haven't had a history of seeing ghosts outside of Pleasant Hill. I don't go to church regularly, although I do consider myself to be a spiritual person. I was a total skeptic when I came here. But too many things have happened here that cannot be explained for me to still be a skeptic. I think the only time I've ever been frightened by a spirit here was when I was coming down the pike from the Trustee's Office. It was during an Elder Hostel, and it was at night and raining. I was walking to the West Family Dwelling. I knew somebody was walking behind me and I could *hear* them. When I turned around, I couldn't see them, so I *ran*. I had heard footsteps and it made the hair stand up on the back of my neck. When I got down the pike by the Farm Deacon's Shop it was gone!

Promiscuous Dancing

Shaker worship was noted for its singing and dancing and channeling of spirits. Sometimes a Shaker worshiper would fall into a trance for days. The devout would thrash and shake out their sins. The group's charismatic expression would build up like a whirlwind. It was like Richard Simmons on spiritual aerobics! Beverly says:

One lady came into the Meeting House. She was visibly shaken. She had stayed in the East Family Sister's Shop. She said, "I have to talk to you, because I think I'm going crazy. Last night at 10:48 (she had written down the time) I heard the most beautiful singing I have ever heard in my life. It was so soft and beautiful, the most beautiful female voice I ever heard. But you know what happened? It got louder and louder and faster and faster. And finally I said, "Why don't you shut up, you're going to wake up the whole building?" And it stopped! And I got up. I should have written down what I heard.

But, the other strange thing is, I didn't understand wha..
singing. It sounded like they were singing in a foreign lan..
I told her, "A lot of times, with Shaker music, the songs will ..
very softly and then they'll get faster and louder. They'll work them..
into a frenzy. It's called 'promiscuous' dancing, like if you'd go to a ..
concert, and get all caught up in the music and feelings."

And the woman said, "Oh, thank God, I really thought I'd lost it.
Since you've said that, I feel much better. Because I thought, whoever
it was, I'd made them angry that I was here."

Randy Folger

Originally from Washington state, Randy was the music director at
Shakertown. He and his family moved to Kentucky when Randy was six years
old, and he started working at Pleasant Hill in 1990. Randy soon became
absorbed in research into Shaker history and theology, in addition to singing
four concerts a day for the visitors. Randy was truly one of the most Shaker-like
employees at Pleasant Hill. His character was gentle and the Shakers' music
became very real when he sang their songs. Randy recorded two albums of
Shaker music and transcribed a Pleasant Hill hymnal into modern notation. He
was a busy worker, performing candlelight concerts, greeting and talking to
the numerous guests who attended the Meeting House concerts, and lecturing
at Elder hostels and schools. In addition, Randy coordinated special events,
workshops, and music programming at the village.

Randy Folger passed on to spirit in 1999. I was in Seattle on vacation,
not far from his birthplace, when I got the news that he had died in a car
accident on the curvy highway near Shakertown. It was hard to accept our
loss. So many people were touched by Randy's
good nature and special gifts. And even though he
smoked cigarettes, I still wanted to be around him,
to just soak up his presence. Randy encouraged
me to collect the Shaker ghost stories. He was very
supportive, and a bit of a ghost hunter himself. In
June, 1998, I went to Randy's home and recorded
his ghost stories. The amazing thing about Randy,
besides my never seeing him get angry, was his
dedication to providing the visitors to the Meeting
House with a unique sound and presence of
someone who was very much Shaker-like.

Randy Folger speaks during
a performance of Shaker
music, Pleasant Hill. *Photo
by Thomas Freese.*

Randy performed the music concerts in the original Shakers' Meeting House. Its foundations are aligned with the Centre Family Dwelling, across the village street, and with the Trustee's Office, which is to the east. The floorboards of the Meeting House have seen and felt the dancing and whirling of the Shakers. The upper floor of the Meeting House had apartments for the ministry (a ruling body of two elders and two eldresses). Like the Centre Family Dwelling across the village pike, the Meeting House has two separate, exterior doors for entry by men and women. The Meeting House is the location of many unusual sights and sounds, heard and felt during both the day and night by employees and visitors to Shakertown.

"Often, I hear of some real weird experiences from the folks who come into the Meeting House for our music programs," Randy told me." Sometimes, people will come up to me to ask questions after I sing and talk to everyone."

Merging Shaker Spirit

Randy said:

One woman sent her family out of the Meeting House and waited until everybody was out of the room. She said, "I just wanted to stick around and tell you something. When you were singing, I saw someone standing next to you. As you were singing, this 'person' got closer and closer to you until; finally, that person was *in* you and singing through you. I saw it just as plain as anything."

Another time, I was doing one of the songs in the "unknown tongue." I was telling the group how the Shakers called that the "angel's language" and that chances are, you wouldn't understand a *word* of that. But this one time that I sang in the unknown tongue, a woman in the front row had the most puzzled look on her face. After the program, she came up to me and said, "You know, I've never been around the unknown tongue, I've never heard anything about it and I don't know anything about the Shakers. But when you said that was in the spirit language, I was floored, because I heard your singing in English."

The woman told me the translation she had heard. It was definitely Shaker sentiments and Shaker theology. This song is over 150 years old and this woman had somehow received a translation! What was odd about this is that, as far as I know, the Shakers are the only denomination that practiced speaking in tongues who would write down the spirit language by phonetics.

Many visitors were entranced by Randy's singing. He delivered the Shaker music program with confidence and humble devotion, and in the question and answer time after his performance, he gracefully fielded a variety of queries about many aspects of Shaker life and worship.

Shakers Still Sing in Empty Meeting House

Randy continues:

I've heard singing in the Meeting House, when there was nobody there. I have heard women's voices and men's voices. I've heard *beautiful* singing. I would hang out and read, in the little closet that had been off to one side, waiting for visitors to come into the Meeting House. As I sat in there, I would hear someone singing and walking around in the main room. But, I'd open the door and there would be nobody there. It was empty. So I knew spirits were there. The Meeting House seems to be the "hot spot" of the village.

I've had other people say that they can hear somebody singing with me at times. They hear another voice, sometimes in harmony.

One time, Randy was in the Centre Family Dwelling, discussing spirit manifestations, when the banister where he had his hand began to shake!

Does Pleasant Hill attract those who are seeking and open to spiritual wonder and metaphysical meanings? Randy tells of a woman who reported being "guided" to come to Pleasant Hill.

She was driving back from a women's conference in Washington, D. C., to her home in California. As she was headed south on Interstate 75, she saw a pillar of smoke or fire. She followed the pillar of "smoke" to Shakertown. She said that the pillar disappeared when she turned onto Pleasant Hill property.

Are those really Shakertown employees, going about their jobs?

Randy said that someone who works at the front desk told of one couple who had reported seeing a man dressed in Shaker garb, chopping wood in the early evening. The guests said, "Boy, you all go to great lengths to provide for an authentic atmosphere." They had seen the man from their room, looking out toward the back of the Ministry's Workshop. But there had been no employee chopping wood!

Randy said:

About three years ago, a friend and I had been through some of the buildings at Shakertown, seeing if we could pick up on the spirits' presence. We were both interested in "ghost busting" and we were very curious as to what sort of spirits could be found. I've always been fascinated by stories of spirits and ghosts and we thought we'd try to find a few ourselves!

We really hadn't discovered much at all, so we started going to the Meeting House. We'd sit there, quietly, to see what might happen. I might sing some Shaker songs to encourage an appearance.

Sometimes we would hear things. I remember one night, it wasn't raining and we heard *drip, drip, drip.* But there's no water in the Meeting House at all. So we had no idea what was causing that, but we could hear it very plainly. Other times, we would hear a footstep or two on the floorboards. But during those spirit searching sessions, we didn't hear anybody singing or dancing. We'd go and sit on the floor to try and connect with the "vibrations." We kept going about once a week. It was kind of fun, though we weren't getting anywhere with our "ghost busting." Sometimes, we'd go up in the attic. There were no lights in there and it was very spooky. We felt, on the second floor, as if somebody was watching us.

A Mighty Wind

Randy's tale becomes more focused:

Then, one night, we decided to go into the Meeting House. It was early fall and about midnight. The weather was calm. We went in and sat for a while. The first thing that we noticed was that one of the windows was totally black. You couldn't see out of it anymore. It was like a blind had been drawn over it. We could see out of the other windows. Even though it was night, we could see the glow of a street lamp or whatever. But at this single window on the west wall that you could normally see out of, it was like there was something in front of it, like it was blocked out. I called it to my friend's attention and I said, "What's that?" And he'd never seen anything like that before. It kind of gave us a weird feeling, like there was something in front of that window.

The next thing we knew, we heard a wind begin to blow in the room. Outside was perfectly calm! It was calm when we went in, and we could look outside the windows and see that the leaves weren't moving. But we could hear this wind, starting up in the room. It started getting faster and faster, and louder and louder. It was circling, like a whirlwind. We both said, "What in the world is going on?" We were getting a little nervous by then, because it was picking up in intensity. It was getting louder and louder, and more violent all the time. I don't recall feeling it on my face. I was hearing it. So we actually got up and just left. We couldn't get out of there quick enough!

I locked the Meeting House door behind us and we came outside. We both walked away, passing in front of the Meeting House. I was thinking, *what in the world was going on in there? That was really a weird experience!* And at that very moment, we heard a roar! To me, it sounded like a werewolf. I know that sounds crazy, but that's what I imagine a werewolf sounding like. It was very low sounding, just beastly. It was not, I guarantee you, a dog, or a coyote, and it wasn't a bobcat. It was right in front of the Centre Family Dwelling, on the other side of the fence, just low enough behind the fence so we couldn't see it. Within a second, we heard it again, but it was all the way down at the East Family Dwelling. It was unreal. That thing was there in front of the Centre Family Dwelling, and the next second it was down at the East Family Dwelling. I don't know how it did it, but this thing moved fast.

The next day I came into work, and Larrie Curry, who is my boss and lives about two or three miles over the hills, said, "Did you notice anything strange, last night? There was a disturbance in the natural world. I could feel it. My animals were going crazy; the dogs and the cats, were all going nuts. There was something going on."

She asked me that out of the clear blue. Whatever we had tapped into, she was aware of it as well.

People, often in rural locations, have reported mysterious crying or screaming animals. In Robb Riggs fascinating book *In the Big Thicket: On the Trail of the Wild Man*, the author provides a number of examples of this odd and eerie-sounding creature. Also see *Tragedy at Devils Hollow and Other Kentucky Ghost Stories* by Michael Paul Henson.

Blue Light Special

Three weeks after Randy died, I had returned to my apartment in Lexington and I believe Randy paid me a visit. I was fast asleep in my bed when I was awakened by hearing my name being called. For some reason, I got up and walked into my spare room where there were wide, sliding-glass doors/windows. What amazed me, despite the obvious source of light from the moon late that night, was that the light was blue. There was no explanation for the blue light. Nothing in the glass or in my room would bend the light from white to blue. I have a lot of experience from childhood as an amateur astronomer, with many hours logged at night observing moon, stars, and planets. I had never before seen the light from the moon appearing in that color. I believe it was Randy visiting and saying farewell. Randy was my blue light special!

Still More Interpreter Stories

Women in White

Debbie Larkin

Shaker women in white attire have been sighted in a few places at Pleasant Hill. One story of a woman in white comes from Debbie Larkin. Debbie was the village herbalist. She is cheerful and bright, and very knowledgeable about the uses of herbs. She teaches classes on the propagation, harvesting, and storing of useful plants, and tended the Shaker herb garden which is on the west side of the Centre Family Dwelling near the central lane. On some of my visits to Shakertown, I would be drawn to the flowers and herbs. I wanted to learn more about herbs and to grow my own. The village, during the prime tourist season, could get a little busy. Those were good times for me to walk down to the lake, stroll out to Shawnee Run Creek, or if I had a shorter amount of time, step off the stone path and take in the beauty of the flowers and herbs. There were sunny chamomile flowers, mint, fragrant lavender, healing comphrey, and much more. I liked Debbie and she was generous with her time and knowledge. And as it turned out, she was in the special club of those who had a Shaker experience.

Call from the Shakers

Debbie says:

My encounter happened three or four summers ago. There had been a woman in the village the day before who was touring Shakertown. She lived fairly close to Pleasant Hill and she offered to donate some mullein and St. John's Wort plants to the village garden. I told her, "Sure, we'd really appreciate it." We have been given many plants from friends to put in the garden. She told me approximately when she would be coming that day. So I was looking and listening for her.

I kept glancing down near the ticket booth from where I was working in the herb garden. It was late morning when I heard someone call my name. I looked toward the ticket booth, and I saw a woman dressed in white, waving at me. I realized that she was making a waving motion with her hand as though she wanted me to come. She was standing in the road near the ticket booth. I waved back at her, but it was too far to shout. So I indicated with my hands that I was coming down to meet with her.

Debbie Larkin at Shakertown, Pleasant Hill.
Photo by Thomas Freese.

I put down my tools and started walking down there, but as I got closer I noticed that nobody was there! I had seen her very near the ticket booth so I went over to it. I asked, "Did you see a woman, dressed in white, with some plants for me?" I just assumed that this was the woman for whom I was waiting. But they said, "No, nobody has been here for a while."

I had seen her standing in the road between the ticket booth and the Farm Deacon's Shop, so I went over to the Farm Deacon's Shop. Again I asked, "Did a lady come in here with some plants for me?"

And they said, "No, we haven't seen anyone."

Then I went into the nearby Craft Store and I asked the shop workers, "Have you seen a lady, dressed in white, with some plants for me?"

They answered, "No, we haven't. It's very quiet here this morning."

Nobody else had seen her!

My friend, the woman with the plants, came later in the afternoon. She was dressed not in a white dress, but in blue jeans and a colored tee shirt. The first thing I said when she arrived was, "Were you here earlier, and dressed in white, with some plants for me?" She said, "No."

This happened during the time when I put a lot of plants out into the garden, late May. That is the time when we often have a lot of students in the village, but there was not much traffic at all that morning.

I told the staff curator, Larrie Curry, about the woman in white. I found out that there was a well-known skeptic of the paranormal who was visiting the village that day, and there was some speculation that the person's presence might prompt an appearance by the spirits.

I felt blessed that they had picked me out to call upon. It had been very quiet around the village, and I was enjoying working in the garden that day. It was a strong impulse that had made me look up and turn to that direction. I wish that I had been paying more attention, but at the time I didn't know that I was having a "Shaker experience." I couldn't make out a face with the woman. I really should have thought it was odd that a woman who was bringing me plants would have been wearing a long white dress. I think that her head may have been covered. But now that I think back, it was almost like an aura, rather than being anything specific.

Other Shakertown employees have also seen mystery women.

Ruth Keller once worked as the front desk supervisor in the Ministry's Workshop building. Even though the upstairs room was locked, she would hear the sounds of someone walking there. She also tells of a night, about 10 or 11 p.m., when a security guard saw a lady at a window on the second floor of the Ministry's Workshop. Ruth stated that she was the only one in that building at that time, and she was downstairs.

Keith Hatter works at Pleasant Hill. He and another worker saw a ghost in the Trustee's Office. Keith reports that a female employee saw a woman with a full skirt going up the spiral staircase and she pointed out the figure to him.

At the West Family Dwelling, guests have reported seeing a woman who is standing at a third-floor window. They had noticed that she hadn't moved from the window for some time, so they inquired about her, thinking that she might need help.

The Shakers Still Sing

Leslie Taylor is one of the many Centre Family Dwelling interpreters. She seems to be the "no-nonsense type," and would not likely be fabricating a story of a spirit. Leslie says:

One morning, as I was coming to work at the Centre Family Dwelling, I walked around the side of the Meeting House as I do every morning. I came in from the parking lot around the east side of the Meeting House. The front door of the Meeting House was open and I didn't think that was unusual. Normally somebody would be here ahead of me to open the door to the Meeting House. This was between 8:30 and 8:40 in the morning.

As I walked around the building, I heard a female voice singing, and out of the corner of my eye I saw the edge of a white dress. At that time, the only person who would have been in there singing was Roberta Burnes. So I didn't think anything about it and walked on to the Centre Family Dwelling.

I told everybody who came into the Centre Family Dwelling that day, "Don't miss the singing performances in the Meeting House, because Roberta Burnes is here and she is absolutely wonderful!"

Well, about three o'clock that afternoon, I left the Centre Family Dwelling to go across the village street. Randy Folger, the music director, came out of the front of the Meeting House. He said, "Now, do *I* look like Roberta Burnes?"

He informed me that Roberta had not been on the property that day! I had heard a beautiful singing voice, but it had not been Roberta.

Sarah Moran, a dining room waitress, reports that:

Last year, a supervisor told me that she had seen a white figure that was kind of floating down the stairs in the Trustee's Office building. She saw it for only a few seconds.

Roberta Burnes might be said to be one of *the* women in white, as she wore a white dress when she performed as a singer. Roberta sang with a powerful and clear voice. She filled the Meeting House with the idealistic feeling of Shaker sentiment through their songs and her singing. Roberta worked part-time as a music interpreter for many years. She once sang and performed Shaker music programs with the Kentucky Humanities Program, and has recorded a compact disc of Shaker women's music. I had been a house sitter in the summer of 1997 for Roberta and her husband, John, when they went to the British Isles. Roberta struck me as a sort of Renaissance person, good with science and also good with the arts.

Choir of Angels

Roberta shared with me that a few times she had been baffled by some invisible accompaniment to her singing.

A couple of years ago, I happened to be singing "Amazing Grace" for a daytime public performance. As I sang, I noticed musical tones contributed by the audience. It was like a choir of angels who were singing "ooo." I thought, *this audience is good*.

After my performance, the folks from the audience came up to greet me and thank me for my singing. They said, "You were really great with that song." And I said to them, "So were you."

But they said, "We weren't singing. There was nobody else singing but you!"

Another time, after that, when I sang "Amazing Grace," I focused on the spirit accompaniment that I again started to hear, but it went away.

Sometime later, I was doing a candlelight performance. I was singing the Shaker song, "The Savior's Universal Prayer." This time it was my husband, John, who heard the choir-like sound, and I didn't hear it at all. When we compared notes, we agreed that it sounded a lot like a choir of women's voices that you hear in those "hokey" old black and white movies, when the voices come in at the end of the film. There had been many layers on top of my voice.

The Mystery of Holy Sinai's Plain

The casual visitor to Shakertown at Pleasant Hill can be easily impressed by the visible achievements of the Shakers. One can see wonderful buildings that are 200 years old, stone fences, a road leading from the Kentucky River, and hundreds of artifacts of an industrious life. Visitors can view the incredible craftsmanship of the spiral staircase in the Trustee's Office and marvel at the organization of the production of various Shaker industries such as, silk, seeds, boxes, and brooms. The Shakers' vibrant spiritual life, however, is a greater challenge to deduce. From journal accounts and visitors' recollections, we know a little of how they danced and sang. They were greatly inspired and tried to live the highest of moral ideals.

On Shaker property, near the main village, lay a mysterious site sacred to the Shakers. This secret Shaker worship site was called Holy Sinai's Plain. This sacred place was long abandoned and the evidence of its existence destroyed by the Shakers. But archaeologists and researchers found the Holy Plain in the spring of 1997. There are a few stories of spirit activity connected with Holy Sinai's Plain and even its discovery. This was the singular location where the "worldly people" could not participate in witnessing the Shaker's worship. The Shakers experienced a charismatic revival from 1837 until 1847. Starting in the community of Watervliet in New York State, incredible visions and spirit personalities were seen. Many of those who became channels for the spirits were young girls—often between the ages of 12 and 15. They were called "inspired ones" or "instruments," and would often speak in the "unknown tongue." This was the angels' language, some of which was recorded in Shaker journals and put into song.

Sarah Pool was the first person of that revival to become an instrument at Pleasant Hill. The messages were consistent with the basic Shaker theology of obedience, humility, repentance, subjugation of the flesh, and orderly life. From their trance state, the inspired ones related messages from Mother Ann and people of the Bible. There were messages from historic men and women: George Washington, Benjamin Franklin, William Penn, Tecumseh, and even God Himself. Invisible gifts would be "distributed" to aid in the worship and in the devotion of the Shaker life: drums, trumpets, fifes, etc.

The Mount Lebanon, New York, community sent out a directive to each Shaker village to set apart a secret worship place some distance from the meeting house. The ministry at Pleasant Hill dedicated a plot of land to be their Holy Sinai's Plain. The Shaker villages had different names chosen for their sacred worship sites. It was noted in the journals as being one-half mile southeast of the Meeting House. Common to these special sites in the various Shaker societies was a leveled spot away from their village, a simple presentation of the sacred circle—the one at Pleasant Hill was sown in bluegrass and had neat, wood fencing—a pool of water and a sacred stone and/or altar.

Holy Sinai's Plain was not visited often. It was for special observances and not open to outside visitors. It is noted that some of the altar stones had a curse carved into the stone advising detrimental consequences for those who might disturb the sacred location. After a period of about ten years, the charismatic guidance that had inspired the revival and the making of the holy ground, indicated that this special time was ending. The villages were instructed to destroy the altar stones, tear down the fence, and to hide all evidence of their location and use.

After his "whirlwind" experience in the Meeting House, Randy Folger decided to stop ghost busting in the Meeting House. One day, he hiked around to investigate the area where Holy Sinai's Plain was reported to be. From Shaker journal entries, some possible locations were looked at on Shaker land that lay on the other side of US Highway 68. Randy and a friend had some baffling experiences in that area of land.

We started going down and looking for Holy Sinai's Plain. We always had to look for these things at night. We'd go down and park on the river road because the gate would be locked. We'd climb over the gate and walk down to the place I used to think was the Plain. We'd go down the road a little way. Right before we'd get into the woods, there was another gate. Then we would climb over the gate and walk up a little hill and there was a beautiful plain.

Shaker Figure Walks Along with Me

One time, when I was walking the old Shaker river road, I felt somebody watching me as I was coming back from the river. This was during the day. I looked back up to the top of the cliffs, and there was somebody dressed in Shaker costume up there, looking down at me. I said, "Hello!" and the person backed away from the edge of the cliff. I walked all the way to the top and I could see this person, whoever it was, over in the line of trees. As I walked, the figure would walk parallel to me. He never would approach me or say hello. I tried to speak to him again. I tried to approach him one time, and he would walk off, into the woods. I have no idea what that was all about.

Randy Folger continues:

The Ouija board can be a little scary sometimes. I don't know how you prepare yourself for what can happen. I remember some of my college mates were doing the Ouija board one night. They said a big wind came up and the planchette took off and flew around the room. It ended up sticking into the wall.

My father told me something very odd that happened to him when I was young, but only told me a few years ago. It was a summer night and all us kids were asleep in bed. He was reading the paper in the living room and heard the door slam as if someone had either gone out of the house or come in. He went to look and saw nobody there so he went to check on us kids.

He said when he looked in my bedroom, he saw a strange woman over my bed with a knife upraised! When he shouted out she simply vanished.

For a while, I got into studying Native American spiritual things. I feel like I sometimes get wisdom messages. Everyday I see Nature changing around me; it's just amazing. I walk here on Shaker property a lot, in the moonlight, watching the stars. I listen to the crickets and the birds. I call this my magic cornfield down here. It's where I seem to get messages. It's close to Holy Sinai's Plain and I see a lot of unusual sights.

One night, I walked down here and there was a herd of deer. They just let me walk close to them. Of course, I wasn't bothering them at all. On the same night, I saw a whole flock of Canadian Geese just sitting there. I walked a little farther and saw something else. Another night, I was walking down to the other field, and, all of a sudden, I heard a waterfall. I thought, *there's no waterfall over there*!

I walked over to see where the water sound was, and, amongst all the weeds, there were all these birds making that rustling sound. Oh, it was just too wonderful. About that time, I looked where I was walking and there was a beautiful hawk feather laying there. So I thought, *this was given to me*. I did a little research and found out that the hawk brings messages.

I used to come here and walk everyday. I've been going over to the old Shaker village and walking the old road a lot.

In addition to seeing the silent Shaker, Randy heard once again from the invisible beast that he and his friend had heard in the village.

On our second night, hanging out at that spot I thought to be Holy Sinai's Plain, all of a sudden we heard a wolf-like growl. It was the same beast that we had heard in the village after the whirlwind in the Meeting House about a week before. It sounded just as loud and just as angry as when we heard it in the village. We had flashlights with us and we shone our flashlights in the direction from which the sound came, but it was nowhere. There was nothing there. It was empty space. The sound had been right there, but when we shone the lights it was gone! Then we heard it again maybe a mile farther off.

My neighbor, who lives two doors down, is a biology teacher at the local high school. He enjoys studying animals. About a week after hearing that wolf-like sound he came to visit me. He said, "Man, I've been hearing the weirdest sounds at night. My wife and I will be sitting out on the patio and we hear an animal we've *never* heard before! I can't imagine what it is." So I don't know what this thing was, but it apparently was down at his house a night or two. If it was indeed an animal; how did it relocate itself to sound out again so quickly? And why would it be close to us to begin with? Usually, animals take off when they hear you coming. My friend actually took someone else to the same spot and they heard this thing too.

Strange Energies

At Pleasant Hill, in our modern era, no physical evidence was found for many years to pinpoint the sacred Plain. But, in 1997, the archaeologists got closer and closer to its discovery. When a worker with a compass crossed over one spot of land, he noticed the compass spinning wildly, then freezing still. The compass, despite some knocks to encourage its regular performance, would not work any more. With bulldozer, backhoe, and persistence, the workers uncovered the "shadow" of the postholes of the Shaker's oval fence that must have surrounded their Holy Sinai's Plain. The posts had evidently been removed, but the soil replaced into those holes was a bit darker. This gave the archaeologists evidence needed to confirm the discovery of the secret worship site. One of the bulldozers would not start up for some time, and in the village itself, some unusual occurrences were noted that day.

That summer I gathered around the trench with other Shaker singers for a photograph for the Lexington newspaper, the *Herald-Leader*. We sang and we tried to project ourselves into the respectful role of latter-day interpreters. But overtime, I heard some intriguing stories of how perhaps the excavation of the site might have upset the Shaker spirits. And later, the singers debated the pros and cons of performing at Holy Sinai's Plain. We had a number of programs where we marched from the village, from outside the Meeting House, to Holy Sinai's Plain, singing all the way. Then we danced and sang at that sacred Shaker site.

Voices Upstairs

Beverly Rogers and two other Shakertown employees had some strange experiences the day of Holy Sinai's discovery. She relates:

> I was doing a Meeting House tour that day. I had unlocked and opened the back door and I was standing in the hallway. I heard voices and walking upstairs. I wondered if Susan Hughes had

brought in some people to show them the attic. I went up to the second floor, but I didn't find anybody. I came back downstairs, getting ready to go into the main first-floor room, and I heard the same thing again. I thought, *maybe they were on the third floor.* So I went back up through the second floor to the attic and I found no one there. When I saw Larrie Curry three or four days later, I told her about this encounter.

Larrie said, "Do you realize that was the day they found the first three postholes in Sinai's Plain?"

Shaker Curse?

Carol Zahn, an interpreter at the Centre Family Dwelling, reports that Larrie Curry and Randy Folger offered a tour of Holy Sinai's Plain to some of the employees. They packed up in cars and drove to the nearby site. Just as they got out of their cars at the sacred site, an unusual sleet storm fell upon them. When they got back to their cars to leave Holy Sinai's Plain, the storm suddenly stopped. Carol questions the strange and isolated storm that fell that day. She wondered if the group had ignored the employee gossip which spoke of a curse that forbade anyone to revisit the secret Shaker site. There had been talk about a stone altar discarded in one of the ponds—an altar which had been carved with a curse to anyone who disturbed Holy Sinai's Plain. Perhaps the Shaker spirits were restless and had not approved of the excavation?

View from a distance of the fence circling around Holy Sinai's Plain, Pleasant Hill. *Photo by Thomas Freese.*

Flying Table

Two Pleasant Hill employees had an astonishing experience when Holy Sinai's Plain was discovered. Rose Sorrell and another employee were in the basement storage room below the craft store. The storage room is reached by descending spiral stairs from the sales floor. The room is narrow with an exit door to the ground level at its end. There is a kitchen table and microwave for employee breaks. And there are long shelves for storing shop merchandise. Rose was standing by the kitchen table, talking to an employee who was about to go out the exit door.

They were discussing some of the spirit world's possibilities, when a small round walnut candle stand lifted and moved through the air. It had been safely stored upside down on the desk. Rose reported that it spun about eight feet across the room and split and broke when it landed. Her coworker was nowhere near the table. A few minutes later, a wooden hanger went flying off from its secure place, bouncing and spinning to the floor.

Rose asked her coworker, "Did you do that?"

He replied, "I don't think so!"

A woman, who is a Centre Family Dwelling interpreter, grew up in the area of Pleasant Hill. She remembers the area of Holy Sinai's Plain feeling different to her and her family.

"When we would walk up to the gate to that area, I wouldn't want to go through the gate and further along there. I got a 'fluttery' feeling."

Reproduction Shaker wooden table. *Photo by Thomas Freese.*

Odd Happenings

The maintenance worker called Tucker reports that "mechanical things go nuts in the two to three weeks before a tour of Holy Sinai's Plain."

Tucker rotates with the other workers on the night maintenance duty.

> Up until two months ago, when the heat got so bad and they canceled the trips to Holy Sinai's Plain, we would be running all night to fix things. The air handlers (heating/cooling systems) would burn out before they were very old. Fire alarms sounded without any fires. Someone would say that there was probably dust or spiders that got into the fire alarm to make it go off. But we'd use an air hose to blow out whatever might be in there, and the air hose wouldn't dislodge anything. There are outside lights on tall poles that we have to get up to with a ladder. We would find those lights up there had been unscrewed. Since the summer heat stopped the tours, we now only get about one or two calls per night.

Tucker added:

> ... just about every worker in the village has turned lights off and later discovered that they would be back on again.

My Aunt was a Shaker

From Jane Beavon:

> My Aunt Sarah was born Sarah Smith in Dayton, Ohio. She married a Stephens man who was also a Shaker. I remember reading a letter once she had written to my grandmother, Elsie Smith Hutsell, saying something about living in a Shaker community in Kentucky. I am not sure where it was because I do not have access to that letter any longer. When Sarah was old, she ended up living in Springfield, Ohio, at the Masonic Home. I know she and her husband are both buried in the Masonic Home Cemetery.
>
> She was a tiny little woman like my grandmother, who was 4'11". I know their mother died due to a miscarriage. She bled to death. Their father, Benjamin Franklin Smith, then gave the children to other families for them to be raised. My grandmother was raised by a Wood or Woods family in east Dayton, Ohio. I guess that was a common practice in those days. The Shakers are fascinating people who have always intrigued me. I just recently discovered another small Shaker museum in Kentucky near Bowling Green which I want to visit some day soon. I was told they have a lot of records of who lived there. I want to research it because it might be where my Aunt Sarah had been at one time.

Shaker singers perform at Holy Sinai's Plain, Pleasant Hill. *Photo by Joel Schulman.*

Author's Note:

It is amazing how many folks have some sort of connection to the people and history of the Shaker village. I did a talk for the Lexington Women's Club, speaking about the ghost stories at Pleasant Hill. My contact there was a very nice lady named Margaret Heaton. When I finished my talk, she presented me with a pretty *thank you* card. The card had a bit of black silk thread pinned to it and a note telling me that it was likely Shaker spun thread, dating to 1912, when her mother had purchased it from the elderly Shaker women at Pleasant Hill.

Shaker artifact—black silk thread from Pleasant Hill, with note, both given to author.

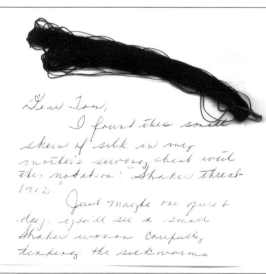

Psychics Visit Shakertown

After collecting a number of ghost stories from the employees and visitors to Pleasant Hill, I was curious as to what sort of information might come from having psychics tour Shakertown. I invited two ladies to travel to Pleasant Hill and we went walking about the village on September 13, 1998. We started in the Meeting House.

Beth Anne Bennett and Wendy B. from Ohio

Wendy:

The women definitely did not have a passive role in the Shaker spiritual expression. I may be tuning into male energy, but I feel that the men sat here on the west side and the women sat over there on the east side. The switching back and forth of assigned or traditional sides was part of working up the energy.

Beth:

There is a woman coming out of the door over there on the east side where the men are supposed to be. The energy in here is really very marvelous. It's wonderful. They did a lot of rocking and rolling. They got the vibrations up very high. You still can feel the vibrations of it—the energetic dance and song. And in that case, they didn't need sex!

Wendy:

I hear beautiful music, bringing in chords and tones and there is chanting. The women definitely played almost a major role. There was a head man, but the women were the focus. The spirit came through them and went into the males. There is a wonderful smell in here. It's not sandalwood, but it's an undertone of fragrance. It's a very soft smell.

Thomas suggests sassafras.

Wendy:

That could be. I see a child up there in the little window. I don't know if that child is supposed to be up there or not!

Beth:

There are also children coming through that door in the corner, on the east side.

Wendy:

I have a feeling that they're watching us.

Beth:

They're peeking in.

Wendy:

Yes, they are definitely peeking in. I want to go stand in the southwest corner over here. I don't know why. There was a male over here, on the visitor's bench. I feel that he was a very important person. He felt like an outsider, but he wanted to join in the Shaker's worship. There was something that held him back, whether it was his prestigious place or something. He really wanted to be out there and participating fully in it. I'm getting that it was a general from the Civil

War era who visited here more than once. I got the name "Frasier." There is a vortex here, more so than I feel from the other corners. The energy comes in and out here.

Beth:

There is a column of white light there; when you talk about it, I can see it.

Wendy:

I lived in an apartment out west that had a column of white light. That's where I would send discarnate entities when they would come, because there were a lot of them out there in Mt. Shasta. And that column was above my refrigerator, which I always thought was kind of funny! I feel that kind of energy here. It's where spirit would come and move out. So this man was really tuned in, he just was afraid to express it. The social norm was more strictly defined back then. But, in some ways, I think that it was more open back then than right now, because the fundamentalists are kind of taking over in this era. I feel a lot of nice, good humor around here. I'll probably take a few back home with me. They did little, funny tricks, though very nice, not mean. There were practical jokers included in this group. Because, by not going through with the sexual part of their mutual affection, they had to show affection and love and caring in other little ways, like little kids do.

Thomas, Tawana, and Suzanne sing some songs to see what the psychics will pick up.

Beth:

When you sang the "Star of Purity" song, I saw a big, muscular gigantic Celtic spirit.

The singers perform "Now's the Time to Enter In".

Beth:

They would get a lot of electricity going with that song.

Wendy:

It reminds me of "Bringing in the Sheaves." It has to do with that kind of harvesting.

The singers next perform, "I'll Reel, I'll Reel To and Fro."

Wendy: (to Beth)

Do you feel this energy right now? It's cooling me off by twenty degrees!

Wendy:

As soon as you started to sing that song, I felt energy. It's a being which I call Isaiah. This same energy comes when someone is speaking the words of Isaiah at the pulpit. The energy is very cool, very electric. It's a feeling that you're safe and peaceful.

They next sing, "Come Love, Mother's Love."

Wendy:

This was one of their favorite songs during the Civil War, because of talking about Mother. I could see a lot of soldiers around the edges of this room who were away from home.

The women sing, "Way Over in the Promised Land."

Wendy:

I heard cracking all over the building. It's not cooling off outside—that's spirit coming through! I know that when angels come through, you'll hear the building cracking like that. There's not a song that is sung in here that doesn't bring forth spirits. It's so active.

They then sing the Shaker song, "Oh, See the Lovely Angels."

Wendy:

I just wanted to say here that about three minutes before, when the young lady said that the angels were here, the energy changed over in this corner and that, indeed, the angels were here. Even though you are doing an enactment—the energy is real.

Beth:

She's beautiful and she's pink!

Wendy and Beth join the Shaker Singers for a funeral reenactment.

Wendy:

Right as the casket was carried into the graveyard, a beautiful butterfly flew up. The energy in the graveyard is very light, and all beautiful. There are no discarnate beings. All of them passed into spirit gracefully during or before the funeral ceremony.

Wendy:

When we first came here and went to the bathroom and flushed the toilet, I had the experience of someone in there, fascinated with the toilet. As the toilet started slowing down, they re-flushed it several times! I feel that it was a male presence in the women's bathroom!

Thomas and the psychics walk into the Centre Family Dwelling.

Wendy:

In the first room on the right we have a male presence who sits in the corner chair, in the big rocker. He is very much a guardian spirit. He actually was rocking for us as we walked into the room. We also have two young women across the hall who were not happy to be here.

Beth:

One of the young women was a very wild child and she wanted to go out and party. There's also a woman over here in the other room in the guy's side.

Wendy:

They're in spirit now, so it doesn't matter which side they're on!

Beth:

So this is the dining room? It feels very happy and lively. They enjoyed this room and they enjoyed eating. They got to talk and interact and be there for each other.
The kitchen feels more serious. They had to go to work in here. But there was a lady, a cook, and she liked to work. She was plump.

Wendy:

She liked to sing here while she worked and I get the feeling that the prayers and love went into the food as they were fixing it. And she really liked what she did! Every aspect of their life was prayerful, like the Native Americans. It went on in harmony all around them. This kitchen was a powerful place. This is where a lot of things got discussed. They were told to get anything out in the open and aired.

The group walks into a small room that is adjacent to the kitchen.

Beth:

This was kind of like a "pass on by" room. Everybody was walking. It's like a trail! I see lots of movement, but nobody ever stopped there much.

The group next walks into the infirmary.

Beth:

There's a very old lady that died in that bed on the right. She was a little short lady with lots of white hair. She had pretty gray, curly hair. She died happy.

Wendy:

Dying was not an unhappy thing here because this is not an unhappy place.

They move up to the Centre Family Dwelling meeting room.

Wendy:

I wonder if they picked up the pipe smoking in the union meetings from the Native Americans, keeping it peaceful, the talking stick.

Beth:

This has a different energy than the Meeting House. It's more grounded and earthy—down to business, to work.

They walk into the weaving room.

Wendy:

There's someone in the rocker.

Beth:

This was a good thing to go into trance with. They were using the body, the feet and their hands, going with the rhythm.

Shaker rocking chair and fireplace. *Photo by Thomas Freese.*

Wendy:

It was very *satisfying*.

The group walks up the stairs in the Centre Family Dwelling to the very top floor.

Wendy:

I'm getting that there were several times they would go up there and just, feel above it all and be by themselves.

The group walks all the way back down into the Centre Family Dwelling cellar.

Beth:

It felt like they did things in precision. There was a teddy bear sitting in one of the chairs. I think they had toys for kids down here.

They walk then into the ministry's dining room and kitchen in the basement of the Centre Family Dwelling.

Beth:

There is a shift of energy approaching the ministry's area. It is more grounded and earthy, a business-like attitude.

Wendy:

It's like, with the Native American shaman who stays apart from the others to stay connected to the Spirit World.

Beth:

Between the two beams there is a vortex of energy; right between there's a column of light coming in here. This is a vortex, where spirit would enter here, to help the ministry in back room.

Wendy:

The feeling is not just from the ceiling fans!

Beth:

The energy from the vortex started here and went wherever it was needed, not just back to the ministry's area.

The group walks up into the loom room, where a female interpreter tells how she had seen a shadow at the loom one time. She reports that the loom pre-dates the Shakers and is from about 1774.

Wendy:

I really felt something and I thought that I saw a shadow, over behind the big loom. I told myself that it could have been a shadow from the nearby trees. That's the only thing that I've ever seen or heard today in the Shaker village. I didn't want to run.

The group walks to another one of the Shaker buildings, the Ministry's Workshop.

Beth:

It has a lofty feel to it. They must have gotten a lot of inspiration from spirit here.

Wendy and the group talk about the soda machine and the front desk's communication equipment, the modern electronic things.

Wendy:

All these things don't seem to be disrupting them, whereas one could get that from other haunts. This is where the power would go amuck, if it did—and I don't feel that it did.

Beth:

It feels very light—lighter than the place where we were downstairs in the basement, the ministry's area in the Centre Family Dwelling. It's wonderful!

Wendy:

It's downright impossible, from our experience elsewhere, whoever starts the religion, it's pure. And then, later, people get in power; after generations the power is abused. What is interesting is that by not having sex and re-propagating themselves, they had built in a spirit that was too pure, so there would be no abuse of power like is often found in sex. The Shaker movement was supposed to just last for a while.

The group walks into the Trustee's Office.

Beth:

The spiral of the stairs really opens the energy field within the self. It opens up the crown chakra.

Wendy:

It was definitely built to open up those that came in from the outside world, in ways that outsiders would not understand, by the beauty and the simplicity. It's the spiral that we now know as DNA. And there are two of them, the double helix. They knew what it took scientists in the 1960s to discover!

Beth:

Did outside people come here to get married? It looked like a bride there on the back staircase...unless she deserted her marriage to join the Shakers. There's definitely a bride coming down those stairs.

Third-floor view downward of Shaker spiral staircase, Pleasant Hill. *Photo by Thomas Freese.*

Wendy:

Look at the sunburst pattern in the wood and window panes. They really knew what they were doing. The founding fathers of this place were working with spirit first, with symbols.

The psychics walk across the village lane to the Water House.

Wendy:

This was a nice cool place to meet in private.

They next walk to the East Family Brethren's shop.

Wendy:

This building feels like a school to me.

The group leaves the village proper to walk a mile to Holy Sinai's Plain, the secret Shaker worship site.

Beth:

There's a circle of beings here. They stood around in a circle where those inner markers are. Does anybody have a pendulum?

Wendy:

There were women Shakers dancing naked here. And everyone in the community wasn't included in this.

The psychics walk into the center of the circular arrangement of Holy Sinai's Plain.

Beth:

It was more select. Oh, there's a lot of energy in here! I see a row of women standing here. I don't know where the men would have been; did they come separately? Well, it would definitely be a place for visions.

Wendy:

You can hear the breeze.

Beth:

You can hear the silence too.

Wendy:

This is what happens when you make a medicine wheel. And the Shakers created the same energetic structure where the Native Americans had the wheel.

Beth:

Yes, I get the impression that they had medicine wheels here before the Shakers were out here…because there's an eagle and an Indian drawing him in.

Wendy:

This is high ground, and yet it feels really protected all about.

Beth:

The Shaker that Randy Folger saw is just the overseer of the land. Union soldiers were out here too.

Wendy:

The Shakers were so in touch with the land that they were like the Native Americans. You don't even want to call them discarnate beings, because they've gone on into the light, and they've come back to be guardians of the land. They loved it so much. These people knew how to go into the light. Most of the people in the audience in the funeral service didn't realize that the Shaker spirits were coming through the actors. Unlike Seth who only came to one person, Mother Ann will come to anyone who will tune in!

Beth:

It's really peaceful.

Wendy:

Yes, you wouldn't have to do anything else, just lay out here in your sleeping bag. Because that's what you do on a vision quest—you go out and you make a specific space and you call in a vision.

Wendy:

And there's some neat people now involved in this. They're not openly religious, they're open! Anyone of those singers in there, it's impossible for them to sing and not be joined by the Shaker spirits. And I think it's true for a lot of singers in general. None of us singers were tied to any one church. Did they do a lot of twirling?

Beth:

When they danced in concentric circles, the inner circle was in movement counterclockwise and the outer circle move clockwise.

Thomas performed a little of "Ezekiel's Vision" song and dance, and noted the concentric and attached circles of dancers.

Wendy:

What you inscribed is a serpent, coiled within itself. It is the kundalini.

Beth:

The Celtic spirit liked it out here.

Many paranormal investigators and organizations employ the services of folks who can be variously described as "sensitive" or "psychic" or a "medium." It is generally acknowledged by our society that there are many among us who have a gift, or have genetically transferred, a different way of knowing what information is obtained in a manner that is beyond material observation and that stretches the boundaries of sensory input. I personally believe, through my experience and in hearing many stories, that we all possess what is referred to as psychic ability, although most people choose to ignore, edit out, and deny that connection with the spirit world. This I think is a determinative construct of the western and mechanistic world view...it is itself, a relatively recent point of view in the ebb and flow of philosophies and spiritual orientation over the history of our planet and its inhabiting mortals. Most people in most societies over most of the history of the world believed, or believe, in dynamic, ongoing, and ever-present interactions and exchange of necessary information with the spirit realm.

What is deliciously ironic is the fact that the original mortal inhabitants of Pleasant Hill knew about their world in the sense of that "different way of knowing." The Shakers daily looked to not only material welfare, but also expected to hear and see and touch the spirit world. Thus, I think it is fitting to have psychics visit Shakertown and share what they see—with that perception we call the second sight, or seeing with the "third eye." I know of four psychics who have visited Shakertown; Randy Folger mentions two other visitors who clearly have that gift. Many who spend a day as a visitor or come for business or stay overnight are in that category of sensitive souls who I would label "psychic attractors." That is, even if they don't make a living giving psychic readings over the telephone or internet, they nevertheless will attract, through sympathetic vibration, or as like attracts likes direct experience with the active and alternate dimension where the Shakers not only continually exist, but also with which they can directly interact.

Some of the information from Wendy and Beth could be seen as psychic imprints, or accessing the images of the typical and historic activities of the Shakers engaged in their daily work or weekly worship. Advanced quantum mechanics and string theory converge at the same location as spiritual teaching—there is no past or linear time; all reality and events happen in the eternal now. What we label alternate dimensions are accessible merely through the power of a mind, a greater Mind which connects with all things. The psychics, and you too, can access that greater Mind and all realities and events if you so choose.

Ghost Hunters
Investigate Pleasant Hill

Danny and Connie Hwang
December 19-20, 2009

Meeting House

During our stay at Shaker Village of Pleasant Hill, Kentucky, my wife, Connie, and I investigated a claim of an apparition seen in the Meeting House. Upon singing the "Angel Shout," described as a "Lo... Lo... Lo" in descending thirds, a man had witnessed a male Shaker figure materialize in front of the benches in a *Star Trek*-like manner. He never dared to attempt that experiment again.

So, I decided to give it a try.

Upon conveying my rendition of the "Angel Shout," I captured an EVP (electronic voice phenomenon) of a female voice sternly saying, "Enough!"

In addition to that EVP, Connie and I both heard a knock emanating from one of the closet doors. Curious, I peeked inside the closet only to find candles, candle holders, and a bag full of plumbing equipment.

Getting no further responses, I decided to leave my digital voice recorder in the room while we toured the west area of the village. Approximately ten minutes after we left, the digital voice recorder captured faint sounds of rustling and footsteps. Shortly afterwards, a breath, very much like a sigh of relief, was recorded on our audio.

I can't say with any certainty that these sounds were paranormal in origin because the audio was not tagged. Tagging is the process of labeling the audible sounds captured during a recording session. Tagging is crucial in paranormal data analysis because it facilitates filtering the ambient or artificial sounds from being misinterpreted as paranormal. Despite this shortcoming, leaving any recording equipment behind can be beneficial in that spirits may be more inclined to express themselves freely once investigators have left the scene.

However, I do know that no one had entered the Meeting House during our absence because the only sounds of the main door opening were when we left and when I came back to pick up the recorder. At that time, I was not aware that the second floor of the Meeting House was accessible. Therefore, it would be misleading to say that the sounds and voices captured on our digital recorder were solely that of spirits. In any case, the Meeting House certainly lives up to its name, for it seemed to be an assembly of possible paranormal activity.

The next morning, I returned to the Meeting House for one final experiment. I employed the use of Shaker music to entice any spirits to my general location. Afterwards, I began a question and answer EVP session.

Bright white orb shows in front of Crafts store door, historic post office at Pleasant Hill.
Photo by Danny Hwang.

Upon asking "Will you pray for me?" I heard and captured a disembodied voice of what sounded like "father…" Could this be one of the Shaker spirits commencing a prayer for me?

Ministry's Workshop

In the Ministry's Workshop, the first floor was used to showcase Shaker-style furnishings for sale to the general public. However, the second floor of the Ministry's Workshop was closed to the public due to renovations. To our dismay, it was on the second floor where most of the paranormal claims were said to occur.

While in the Ministry's Workshop, Connie and I separated to visit the rooms on the first floor. Later on, as Connie was examining the Shaker-crafted furniture in one of the rooms, she heard footsteps on the second floor. Assuming it was me, she walked down the hall towards the staircase. However, she paused at the bottom of the staircase because the steps were closed off with a velvet rope and sign stating "Employees Only." She called out my name to see if I was upstairs. To her surprise, she saw me walk out and address her from one of the other first-floor rooms.

Centre Family Dwelling

There have been claims that an apparition of a young girl was seen in the cellar of the Centre Family Dwelling. So I gathered some equipment and went to the cellar early the next morning. Camcorder in hand, I stopped to sit on a bench to conduct an EVP session.

I set my camcorder down on the bench space beside me. And there it was. On the left staircase of the Centre Family Dwelling cellar stood a translucent gray outline of a girl staring in front of where I was sitting.

The apparition of this girl appeared to be wearing a Shaker-style dress. Her right arm was positioned in a 90-degree angle as if clutching something against her chest. Suddenly, an orb of light began fluttering erratically around her upper torso area and then she vanished.

Centre Family Dwelling, Pleasant Hill. *Photo by Thomas Freese.*

120

Trustee's Office (Room 305)

Before dinner, Connie and I introduced ourselves to the spirits and offered gifts in the form of perfume and a toy squirrel. During setup, I placed a camcorder in a corner of the room to record any activity during our absence. Upon returning an hour later, we found the squirrel knocked over onto its side. Replaying the footage, we discovered that sixteen minutes prior to our return, the squirrel started tipping ever so slightly by itself until it fell completely over onto its side.

We later disregarded this phenomenon as paranormal because prior to the squirrel falling, we heard heavy footsteps walking towards and away from our door. We tested to see if the event could be duplicated with me simulating the heavy steps. Sure enough, the vibrations from my stomping triggered the squirrel to tip over.

Throughout the night, our camcorder captured several orbs of light floating across the room. In one particular instance, we played a Shaker song, "Music of Angels," to attract any spirits to our vicinity. Just thirty-four seconds into the song, a pulsating orb of light was caught floating from the dresser towards my head.

In addition, we kept hearing what sounded like a dog barking outside. I got up to peer out the window to see if I could pinpoint its origin. I later discovered that it was merely the wind blowing on the shutters. But during my time peering out the window, our camera's audio captured an EVP that sounded like a male whispering.

With reports of a lady apparition in period dress seen walking down the rear spiral staircase in the Trustee's Office, we decided to venture to the third floor during our investigation. Rather than aggressively hound the spirits with stabbing questions, we employed a more passive approach this time around. Connie and I sat at opposite ends of the floor and simply engaged in conversation with one another. We tried this to pique the curiosity of any spirits in the hopes of catching them eavesdropping on our conversation. It appeared this non-intrusive method proved quite effective.

During our hour long conversation, the microphone on our camcorder captured three EVPs. The first EVP sounded like a little child interrupting our conversation with what sounded like "is he" or "busy." A second EVP was registered five minutes later, of a woman greeting us by saying "Welcome to Pleasant Hill." Just four minutes after this EVP was captured, I was commenting on the many versatile uses of the Shaker wall pegs, when all of a sudden that same female voice interjected in an inquisitive tone "good?" Lastly, an unusual orb of green light flashed for merely a second right above one of the staircase railings on the third floor.

"Whitehall"

"Whitehall" of the Trustee's Office is aptly named because the entire hallway is painted white. There have been reports of service technicians feeling as if someone were watching them. In addition, people felt someone tap them on their shoulders. But upon turning around, there was no one there. So Connie and I went upwards to investigate these claims.

While in Whitehall, we kept hearing sounds of furniture being moved across the floor. This sound was even heard while we were downstairs in our room hours earlier. But we attributed it to the actions of guests next door. However, when we heard that sound again at 2:05 in the morning, we began to wonder if it was our neighbors downstairs.

One technique I have adopted to facilitate the communication with the paranormal is to use the knocking system. I would inform the spirits that one knock on a table or wall signified "yes," while two knocks communicated "no." During our investigation in Whitehall, I asked if they wanted us to leave. Seconds later, we both heard one knock.

So we decided to leave a digital voice recorder in Whitehall overnight. This turned out to be a brilliant idea because not only did we capture additional sounds of furniture being moved throughout the night, but we also captured what sounded like a male grunt immediately following the sound of furniture being moved, and two EVPs.

Though we could not discern the first EVP captured at 3:37, the second EVP, captured at 4:40 a.m., was alarmingly clear. The voice was that of an agitated man telling someone to, "…come HERE!" Curious, I asked the front desk as to what time the morning shift employees made their way in. Her reply was, "6-7 a.m."

Later that morning, I went back into Whitehall to retrieve my digital voice recorder. I also brought with me a CellSensor EMF detector. This device has an attached sensor that is calibrated to detect electromagnetic fields (EMF). I brought this device to measure the levels of EMF in Whitehall because exposure to high levels can result in the same symptoms experienced by the service technicians (i. e., paranoia and feelings of being watched). I discovered that the light fixtures and a nearby breaker box in Whitehall emitted high levels of EMF (+10 milligauss). Were these high levels of EMF the sole cause for feelings of being watched as experienced by the service technicians? Perhaps not, but it could be one possible mechanism.

Activity While Asleep?

During our sleep, the camera's audio captured two more voices at 6:45 and 6:53 a.m., respectively. It was during one of my snoring melodies that a male voice was captured saying, "Wow... stay at home."

Eight minutes later, that same voice said, "Oh, what a day…"

I did not include these last two voices as evidence because I could very well have been talking in my sleep. The voices captured were awfully clear and crisp. In most of the EVPs that I have captured, the voices are often faint and have a resonating quality to them.

I do admire the dedication of ghost hunters, who are willing to lose sleep and risk a certain amount of body safety, as they walk through decrepit old structures in search of evidence of those who exist without a solid body. While some of their technological instruments may be in the earlier stages of development, I think they advance societal acceptance of the dead being active within our normal sphere of reality. As long as ghost hunters and layman alike acknowledge that the investigator affects the investigation, then we can objectively sift through the collected video, audio, and other digital results.

Meeting House, Whitewater Shaker Village, Ohio.
Photo by Thomas Freese.

123

I have met many ghost hunters who seem to me to be normal folks with a curious bent. I've walked on just a few investigations, not a lot of hours, but enough to follow their earnest efforts as they work anything from a casual walkthrough with handheld electronic meters, voice recorders, and cameras, to a more comprehensive layout of equipment—a sort of paranormal stakeout. I think the ghost hunters were the first ones to identify many sources of "false anomalies," that is, odd images on film/prints and digital photos which can be falsely assumed to be created by discarnate energy or spirit. This healthy filtering and rational skepticism which the average ghost hunter possesses is very helpful for our reasoned assessment of that gray area of so-called paranormal events. This self-censoring is obvious in the comments made in this foregoing chapter by Danny Hwang, who notes the plausible limits and possible contaminating sources of sounds recorded.

There are many historic sites where ghost investigations are not allowed, or variously, are selectively permitted or done in secret by either hosting historical location or ghost hunter groups or both. What has been frustrating for investigators of both story and digital evidence of haunted locations is to deal with conspiratorial silence, or worse yet, blatant verbal assertions, (that I would label lies), such as, "Our (*fill in the name of the historic site*) is not haunted." Curiously, that statement by the representative of the historic location does not match firsthand accounts on that same location related by visitors, docents, volunteers, guests, maintenance workers, newspaper reporters, photographers, lower-level employees, psychics, and the general public. And that general public is becoming increasingly convinced by experience and by the overwhelming evidence throughout our haunted land.

What "they" don't tell you is that:

- You are dining in a restaurant that was once a morgue.
- Your children are playing in a location which was once a pioneer cemetery.
- You've purchased a house where someone committed suicide.
- You got a great deal on the purchase of a Victorian house because the previous residents are desperate to escape paranormal activity.
- The cornfield outside your pretty country home reveals rectangles of sunken earth.
- When the school community has gone home for the day, the maintenance workers are seeing children's ghosts in the hallways and library.
- Your resort community is built on a Native American burial site.

- Your golf course was a Civil War battlefield.
- The parking lot for the municipal building was a former spot where Confederate soldiers or guerillas were executed by hanging.
- That pretty, grassy sloping historic road leading to the river is where chained slaves were marched downriver.
- The charming antique rocking chair you purchased for $100 comes with more than quaint provenance.
- The stone pavers leading to your mobile home, when flipped over, are revealed to be gravestones from the eighteenth and nineteenth century.
- A certain but small percentage of the overnight guests in your bed and breakfast are scared enough to check out and never come back.

I am not making up any of the above situations. They all come from researched and reported firsthand experiences of people who I have interviewed, or from the stories provided by other authors, from not only old Shaker villages, but from a range of locations across Kentucky and in other states as well.

We, as a society, minimize, deny, or actively suppress the information of not only the significant and traumatic events at our historic sites, but the energetic/spiritual realities or at least psychic/emotional ramifications of those events. In other words, the lives of those who came before us, are not dead and gone. And, thankfully, we have paranormal researchers, authors, and ghost hunters, to bring sanity and perspective to the grand disconnect between what we genuinely see, hear, and feel, and the (to be overly generous) mis-speaking of institutional and business "authorities." Presumably these organizations have their rationale for the conspiracy of silence and outright denials. However, I would state this following bit of wisdom, which I consider true for individuals and I think would also hold true for organizations who are caretakers of historic and haunted sites. Once you set aside honesty, you lose integrity.

Conference Attendees Report Ghosts

So what do the "common people" report concerning odd incidences in their overnight stays at Pleasant Hill? One set of online posts from a convention held a few years ago yields some first hand reports, which will be detailed below. ALEP (acronym for A Long Expected Party) 1 Convention was held in 2008 at Shakertown. Pleasant Hill hosts many conferences, meetings, and reunions. It is interesting to discover online postings for some of these gatherings—accounts which certainly seem to indicate that the Shaker village is active with more than mortal visitors.

One lady stayed in the West Family Dwelling, alone in her room and spoke of an incident on Saturday evening. She saw the light in her other and larger room flicker out. When she determined that there was not a wall timer which could explain the light going out, realizing that there was not an overall power outage, she suspected an alternate explanation. At that moment, the light flicked back on, seeming to be a sign from the spirits that she was not really alone and that brought her, she said, "a sense of peace and calmness."

Another woman who stayed at the Tanyard, on the other side of the Shaker village, was upstairs alone on Friday afternoon. The rest of her party had left for group activities, while she had tarried there to get better organized. After she finished, and latched the bedroom door to leave, she went downstairs to gather a few more of her things on the way to her car. She then was surprised, saying, "I heard the door to the bedroom upstairs open and close, followed by footsteps walking down the narrow hall and starting downstairs." I am amazed that she didn't immediately turn tail and run away! But she stood fast, hearing the footsteps fade away before reaching the bottom of the stairs. She reported, "I didn't feel frightened per se, but rather as though I had been accidentally eavesdropping on someone else's business for a few minutes." She walked over to the base of the stairs, just to have a look upwards. Of course, there was nobody in view.

Another convention participant, who didn't detail the specific spot on the village, had a fitful sleep on Thursday night. When they awoke about four in the morning, they sensed a presence in their bedroom.

I didn't see anything because I never opened my eyes...but I felt that there was a female, mother-type spirit sitting on the edge of the bed, showing a younger, toddler-type spirit how to observe us without disturbing us too much. It was entirely benevolent, even sweet in a way, but still a little unnerving, and I didn't actively acknowledge it before letting myself drift off again.

Shaker hallway, stairs and windows. *Photo by Thomas Freese*

One woman, along with a number of her convention mates, had a firsthand encounter. She didn't identify the building but reported that they were doing kitchen cooking duties and the location had a basement. She and another person were chatting when they heard a shuffling noise. It seemed to originate in the basement.

> I heard more shuffling, and the sound of something being knocked over, but we were the only ones in the building, and it was locked tight.

They promptly left, but the lady then took the keys, and her recent experience/story, to the employees working in the building next door. The ladies there said that a similar event had happened the night before, although they had actually seen a ghost.

> He was an older gentleman with a beard, and cold, dark eyes.

She related that the employees were afraid to go upstairs to finish their work. The convention lady then went along with the two workers, who completed their chores. But they noticed a door which had been closed was now open. Also, the visitor then heard sounds like rattling and shuffling from the bathroom. She saw a brief shadow move past.

> My heart beat in my chest. I told her to look but she hesitated before finally looking in... Soon thereafter, the noise got louder, much louder, and the shadow returned. This time she saw it! With a scream, she fled downstairs. I closed the door and followed suit.

Despite their firsthand encounter, one of the two employees reportedly accused the convention lady of creating the strange noises. She returned to protest her innocence when another scream came from one of the workers.

> I burst in the door, and both were standing before me, pale and terrified.

The workers then reported that, as one employee had her back to the other, speaking outside the window, a ghostly Shaker man had appeared and "glared at her with dark eyes." She explained that her scream made the specter disappear.

The final segue to this series of incidences involved the night security employee showing up and affirming that the local lore indicated that there was a Shaker spirit who watched over that building and who they called Isaiah.

Her posting the bizarre set of experiences concludes:

> I know sleep will evade me this evening, and when it does come, it shall be filled with stuff of nightmares.

The Ghosts of White Water Shaker Village Ohio

White Water Shaker Community was formed in 1824 and ended in 1916. More than twenty original Shaker buildings still stand, having been purchased by the Hamilton County Park District from private owners in 1989-1991. White Water is one of 24 communal villages founded between 1787 and 1824 by the United Society of Believers in Christ's Second Appearing, generally called Shakers. It is the only one of four Ohio Shaker villages retaining most of its original buildings in their original settings. The village is located twenty-two miles west of downtown Cincinnati and five miles from Interstate 74 in the Miami White Water Forest, Hamilton County Park, near Harrison, Ohio, on Oxford Road between New Haven and the Butler County line.

The nucleus of the White Water settlement formed in 1822 when members of the Union Society of Shakers from Lebanon, Ohio, came to share their religion with a group of settlers living near the Mt. Tabor Methodist Church, Morgan Township, Butler County. They soon found rich soil, abundant timber, and the flowing stream of the Dry Fork of the White Water River in Hamilton County, Crosby Township, and established the Village there. Early converts donated their properties, thus enlarging White Water's holdings. Intensity of religious fervor motivated construction of the first permanent brick structure, the meeting house, in 1827, followed by a large dwelling in 1832, then workshops, a trustees' office, barns, corn cribs, milk houses, smokehouses, a mill, and other dwellings. Crops of broom corn were the first to be planted, from which brooms were assembled for commerce. The Shakers thrived with sales of seeds, brooms, fruit products, wheat, sorghum, and livestock. As a communal society, no property was individually owned. All members participated in labors for the good of all. A principle of Shaker beliefs is celibacy. Shakers depended on attracting converts and adopting orphans. Following the Civil War, village population waned as strict Shaker religious practices lost appeal in favor of the liberal ways of the "world." Industrial manufacturing reduced the market for handmade goods; the Shaker seed market declined and was discontinued at White Water. Farm labor had to be hired from the outside neighborhood. A fire, in 1907, destroyed the largest dwelling, a popular elder died in 1910 after a prolonged illness, and the Shaker school was closed; this all contributed to the demise of the community of White Water.

The parent ministry at Canterbury, New Hampshire, sold White Water to private owners, prompting the last two Shakers to depart from Harrison in 1916. The Shakers of White Water Village were officially commemorated by the placement of a large white stone memorial by the Canterbury Ministry in the center of the village cemetery. The marker honors all the Shakers who had lived and died there. For the next seventy years, the former Shaker farms provided livelihood to several independent families. The cemetery was neglected until 1984 when two individuals restored it, and it is now the responsibility of Crosby Township Trustees to maintain. The school was razed to make room for cultivation. The great cow barn was dismantled for building materials. The Center Family west bank barn was struck by lightning and burned. The granary at the South Family burned. The North Family bank barn was neglected until it collapsed.

The Hamilton County Park District purchased land between 1989 and 1991 to expand the Miami White Water Forest in northwest Hamilton County. About 600 acres included in the purchase had once belonged to the Shakers, and there stand more than twenty Shaker-built structures that comprised the White Water Shaker Community. The Park District removed post-Shaker structures and stabilized, cleaned, and painted the remaining buildings. Due to the Park District's mission to focus on outdoor recreation and preserve land and habitat for wildlife, the South Family was leased to the University of Cincinnati for an agricultural research station, and the North Family was leased to the Friends of White Water Shaker Village for restoration as a historic site. The Center Family remains in a mothballed state. Presently, the Shaker meeting house is being restored by the Friends, with the goal of opening the North Family to the public by 2014. They believe that the village is an important part of the cultural heritage of America and should be open for all to learn about Shaker communal history, their place in American architectural history, and the importance of preserving examples of our past.

Source (used with permission): http://www.WhiteWatervillage.org/

At the White Water Shaker Village, a woman rented the Meeting House. She and her children had their bedrooms upstairs.

She worked for the Hamilton County Parks and her presence in the old Shaker building helped keep the place secure. But she had odd things happen when she lived there. Someone joked with her that she encountered an angry male Shaker spirit because her bedroom was on the south side, which was the men's half of the Shaker building.

Carol claimed that a voice she heard calling her name often sounded right in her face as she slept. More than once, as she left the building, she looked back and saw a shadowy silhouette in the window to the stairway. Inside, she also heard loud banging noises which circled around on the doors and windows.

Once, her children had muddy shoes they left downstairs. In the morning they came down from their bedrooms to discover that someone had cleaned the shoes. She actually caught sight of the Shaker male. She said he was an elder with a long, dark cloak.

In 2008, Jim Innis, who with Rich Spence have been active with the Friends of White Water Village, both were perplexed by an incident at one of the White Water Shaker buildings.

Last week, Rich Spence and I approached the north door to the Meeting House. I turned the key in the lock but the door wouldn't budge. I tried again, and pushed hard on the door, but it seemed to be held from the inside at the top, where there had been a sliding bolt. I had removed that bolt when we had the new security system installed, but for the moment I thought someone must have reinstalled the bolt. We walked around to the south door, opened it and I disarmed the security system, then stepped toward the north door but it then gently swung open to my touch! Rich and I were astonished!

Rich Spence also reported on some curious going-ons.

Trustee's Office at Whitewater Shaker Village, Ohio. *Photo by Thomas Freese.*

On August 1st, 1993, I went in the morning to the White Water North Family Dwelling to take paint samples. I took some photos of the Milk House and studied the siding. I had arranged to meet the ranger there at 10 a.m., but when he didn't arrive, I asked the tenant, Carol, to let me in. In the dwelling, I took samples from the window frame.

Carol came in then, telling me that her son had seen the ghost two mornings ago. He had been downstairs, in the Meeting House, lying on the couch, when at 5 a.m., he woke up to see a tall Shaker brother looking at him. He told her that the Shaker brother was dressed in a dark suit with a white shirt. He said that the ghostly Shaker then walked into the "bathroom" or closet under the south staircase.

I continued after that to take more photos, not thinking much of the ghost stories. I changed film in the garret north room. I wished I had the lens cap, which was *not* in my pocket. Later, I saw the lens cap on the workbench in the first-floor hallway. When I got ready to leave, I gathered up my stuff which I had left on the workbench. I took off the flash and looked for the lens cap. Well I couldn't find it because it turns out it was now on the camera! I <u>swear</u> I didn't put my lens cap back on the camera, as I had just come downstairs and only had time to take off the flash. Was the Shaker brother playing a prank on me?

The North Family dwelling had a cemetery which contained both pioneer and Shaker graves. It was down at the creek and many tombstones were simply fieldstones. But it has been reported that a developer in the 1990s simply bulldozed the stone markers into the creek. Perhaps the Shaker and other spirits are unhappy and searching for their lost resting places. Once, when the park patrol came by the Shaker place, a neighbor asked if the officer had seen anything unusual. The neighbor told him at night he had seen a Shaker elder with a boy looking out the window. But the officer claimed the place was always locked and with active alarm system. At the old Minges House, which was the White Water Shaker Centre Family Trustees Office building, a ranger came to check on the house, disarming the security system to walk inside and check things out. But he heard children's voices, so he walked about to find out the source of the sound.

He checked all the rooms and doors and there was not another living soul. He still heard the voices of children playing. So he decided to talk to the spirit children, "Are you all having a good time?"

But then he felt foolish, so he said loudly in anger to himself, "This is stupid!!" Immediately he heard a door slam very loudly. He left quickly. He said there was no open door or breeze that would have caused the door to slam like that.

My Friend Lived in a Haunted Shaker House

Joy Walters tells this story:

The park where I work owns a few Shaker Houses, known as the White Water Shaker Community. One of my best friends used to be a tenant in one of the houses several years ago. This particular house was used by the Shakers as the Meeting House. My friend told me several stories over the years of what she and her family had experienced while living there. I too, had something unexplainable, or explainable, depending on how you look at it, happen while there visiting her.

The house was typical of a Shaker dwelling, having a staircase on either side of the house. There was a certain side of the house, to include the stairway, that was the "bad" side of the house. As you would face the house from the front, the "bad side" was the one to the right, or the north. My friend hardly ever used that side of the house, and she even blocked off the stairway on that side.

On a few different occasions, they used the "bad side" when company came over because that was where her formal living room was located. She has several photos that were taken of people on that side of the house with oddities in the photos. There is one of a friend, who has three wispy rings completely encircling her body to include one around her neck, one around her shoulders, then the last around her mid section. Another photo I remember seeing was of my friend sitting in a formal chair that was located closest to the "bad stairway." In the photo, you can see a cloudy looking apparition of a tall man standing behind the chair with his hand on her shoulder. I am sure this was not the case of something wrong with the film negatives.

My friend told me that on several occasions, her neighbor from across the street would call her at work and tell her that the front door on the right, the north of the two side-by-side front doors, was standing open. Carol, my friend, said that neither she, nor her family, ever used that door, and that they left it locked at all times. Carol also told me that one night she was awakened by a man's voice which sounded very loud and stern. He shouted to her, "Blessed be thy son!" She also told me of a story that was relayed to her where the Deacon of the Shakers actually sat up during his funeral and gave his own eulogy.

I thought the world of my friend, but I never liked going over to that house. I felt she was right in sensing something wrong with the right side of the house and I sensed it, too. Even her young children felt it. Her four-year-old daughter had a "playmate" that would come over and play with her. She "lived" down the road a little ways. Carol's daughter described the girl to Carol, to include the very old style of clothing she wore and her name. I remember the name was an old name, not a very commonly used name these days.

Whitewater Shaker Broom Shop, Ohio. *Courtesy of the Library of Congress.*

Getting back to the "bad side" of the house, and the "bad stairway," my biggest, and most frightening experience there was one evening when I had to go to the attic with some furniture. I brought along a police officer friend of mine to help me to move it. He did not believe in ghosts. We carried the furniture to the second floor. Then we had to go over to the north side of the house and continue to the attic using the bad side. I started to get an uneasy feeling as soon as I hit those stairs, and the closer to the attic I got the worse it became. I hit the attic, and had to leave. There was just a very bad feeling up there. Once we were done, Carol started to explain to my friend that the Shakers were a very clean type of person, that "Cleanliness was next to Godliness" in their eyes. He had to poke fun, and as soon as he cracked off with, "I can see it now... I feel as though someone is washing my hair!" we all heard a very loud thud! We took one look at each other, each one of us wide-eyed, and out the door we all ran, into the darkness outside in the backyard! Well, being the macho cop that my friend thought he was, he reluctantly decided to go back in and investigate. He said that there must be a logical explanation. I, too, am a cop, but I certainly was not in a hurry to go back inside! I knew what the explanation was. Anyway, once inside we discovered a shaving kit bag at the bottom of the "bad stairs." Carol said that the shaving kit bag which had fallen was wedged between two large pieces of luggage at the top of the stairs. My other friend suggested that her cat must have somehow dislodged the shaving kit bag and knocked it down the stairs. So, we told him to go up to the top of the stairs to see if it would make the same loud thud if it were to roll down the stairs. There was no loud thud. He tossed it, and still, there was no loud thud. He threw it as hard as he could. It still was not as loud as when it came down the first time. I think it made a believer of him. I know it did the rest of us.

Centre Family Wash House, Whitewater Shaker Village, Ohio.
Courtesy of the Library of Congress.

Odd Pictures
Tina O'Connell relates:

I have driven by the White Water Shaker Village meeting house and dwelling house many times and I always wanted to go inside because I love historic buildings. While having drinks with friends one night in March 2001, I learned that the two buildings are owned by the Hamilton County Park District and that a park district employee was living in the meeting house. I got her telephone number and called to see if I could get a tour.

In the course of our conversation, the tenant, Julie, told me she had heard of several ghostly encounters experienced by previous tenants and that she was hoping to have an experience herself. A few weeks later, Julie and I arranged a small gathering of "ghost hunters" with the hope that something would happen. Complete with Ouija board, we toured the meeting house, took many photos and waited. Nothing happened, although a few of the men claimed they felt uncomfortable on the women's staircase.

However, when I developed my photos, I discovered several strange, three-dimensional images on the landing of the north or women's staircase. The photos were taken on the women's staircase, on the right side of the house if you're looking at the front. I took photos looking up the stairs, looking down the hallway toward the stairs, and from the landing in the middle of the stairs. I did some research on the Internet and learned that ghosts don't always manifest in human form. The images in my photos were similar to other spirits caught on film.

To me, and others, there seems to be a 3-D zigzag type of light on the landing, and random lights that don't seem to be reflections of anything. There were no lights on when the photos were taken and most were taken during the day. We checked and couldn't figure out what could cause any type of reflection. I think we covered up the windows. I don't know if you can see the weird light thing on the ceiling in the hall. It looks like a water reflection but there was no water nearby and wavy window glass wouldn't reflect like that.

We tried to be scientific about taking photos to eliminate any type of light source. I did take similar photos of the other (men's) staircase and nothing showed up like on the women's stairs. The photos were taken at the same time and the stairs are mirror images of each other. There are no trees in front of the house to affect the light, either.

Odd photographic image, Meeting House, Whitewater Shaker Village.
Photos by Tina O'Connell.

Psychic Walkthrough at White Water Shaker Village, Ohio

Ann Richer, Spiritual Counselor from Cincinnati, Ohio,
Accompanied by Thomas Freese

Ann begins:

To the immediate right of the tank you can see the boss tree of this area. I'm going to go talk with that tree for a little while.

There is a whole group here. There are also a lot of psychic imprints here. I'm working on sorting out what are imprints and what are actual spirit presences. I'd like to go inside this room and sit down. I'm on the second floor of a Shaker building. I'm looking at a room with a lot of chairs in it.

I thought about sitting in the closest chair but I got a message from a female who said, "Don't sit in my chair!"

I think I'll sit in the chair with the re-woven seat, just to show respect for the ones who don't want me to sit on their stuff. It seems like this community shut down about 1924. I'm seeing various numbers of inhabitants. There were between twenty-three and twenty-eight individuals who were here for most of the time. Then it started dwindling, about 1915, before people moved away, left or died.

This section is in the meeting house.

Thomas sings some Shaker tunes.

By singing that song, you activated a lot of psychic imprints, here where they had a whole lot of fun. I'm seeing a lot of long, dark dresses with white aprons and little white cap things. There is one female who was very impressed with Catholic nuns so she wore a longer white thing that went halfway down her back with a bill on it. Everybody let her do that but nobody followed that dress style.

The women's apron straps crisscross in the back and a lot of them were just kept scrupulously clean. There was an enormous amount of energy put into washing these clothes and keeping them clean and well-pressed. They used something that would stiffen the clothes, like a starch. I don't know if starch was available then but there was something they used to keep it nice and stiff looking.

There are a lot of dancing and singing psychic imprints left in this building.

I noticed in the other house upstairs a piece of equipment with a name of a man called Ezra on it. He is here although he has crossed over and I am basically channeling him now. He's a very sweet man, very happy to come and help, very interested in this. This is cool to him. So he's happy to talk with me. He enjoyed singing, although he didn't like his own voice so he sang softly. He couldn't carry a tune very well but he enjoyed it a lot. And he enjoyed you singing that Shaker song right now.

He did a lot of preaching here, a lot of talking. He was more of a gentle soul. He didn't like being a boss but rather encouraged, supported, and helped keep it as a community. He wasn't a dictator type. He didn't like to be overly strict.

It seemed that they didn't have much problem with people getting out of line in terms of behavior. They didn't have a need for discipline or putting anyone in jail or banishing anyone. It was a very inclusive sort of thing. It attracted more of the older souls. There were a few younger souls here but most of them were more mature who participated in this.

Thomas sings another Shaker song.

It looks like there was not much touching between male and female. So when they danced they were just to themselves, not holding hands. When these people danced, they were pretty much tuned into themselves and the music as opposed to interacting with each other. Of course, they were aware enough so they didn't smack into each other. But mostly they were tuned inward to experience the rhythm and the beat. It was a dancing meditation basically.

That Ezra guy and two other men liked to tell stories. So there was a lot of storytelling in here in addition to the preaching and singing. They taught the children in this room. They taught the kids how to cook and do carpentry, to build things and keep the place going. It seems there was a large wagon here with big wheels. They are telling me that it was sold. They used the wagon to move earth, hay, woods. At one time there were two horses here but otherwise they pulled the wagon themselves.

They had some skilled woodworkers. There were neighbors in the area, in the surrounding farms, not like there are now. Some of the neighbors didn't like this place; they hated it, thought it was bad, evil. They resented the Shakers. When they went past they would throw nasty energy at it. The Shakers were not vindictive in turn but it did make them feel sad. They would just be sad about it, no attempt to get back at them or fight.

Thomas sings another Shaker song.

This group came together mostly from about a fifty-mile radius. There was some traveling out and Ezra did a lot of it just to find people to interact with and to trade with. There were two other men who did that also. The women mostly stayed here. But the men brought in like-minded people and that's how they gathered. It was a group soul agreement that they would do this.

I'm seeing one who came from Minnesota and settled in Indiana. The Shakers made contact and he joined. But the rest of them were pretty much born in a fifty-mile radius. There were a few from Kentucky.

There were a couple of very talented musicians, real good guitar players, and singers. One was a real good piano player but there wasn't a piano here. They would have liked to have one to play but that wasn't available. They had cows part of the time. There was a veterinarian who wasn't a Shaker himself but felt very much goodwill toward the community and he tended to the animals when they needed that kind of help.

This was not only Shaker ground but there were Native Americans before the Shakers took over. The Indian spirits kind of still hang out here and keep the energy real nice. There's a small vortex over there. [Ann points to a northwest corner of the Meeting House.] The Native Americans used to hang out there.

Ezra was a Native American in another lifetime and that's how he found out about this land. He was a part of the tribe that once lived here. Part of the negative energy I have felt here is a remnant from those non-Shakers who passed by as they thought, *there is something wrong with these Shakers... They must be bad...* That negative energy remains in some of the psychic imprints.

Ezra says he has done a lot of work to help the souls who are here to cross over. He'll be happy to assist because some of them are happy to get through to them. A lot of them like hanging out here because of the love of the land. They loved their lives here, they loved the energy here, and they felt at peace here. They feel like they're caretakers.

What happens with a vortex is very similar to breathing. We breathe in clean air and we breathe out carbon dioxide. On the inside where the vortex comes up, usually, that energy is very positive. And it stirs up the negative energy on the outside. It is not wrong or bad or evil, just unpleasant human energy. That is pretty common.

I am seeing raccoon spirits, groundhog-type animal beings. I wonder if they've found animal droppings in these buildings. I'm communicating with a few women now, but Ezra is coming through the most. Most of those Shaker spirits have crossed over. I don't feel there is a lot of trapped energy here. Ezra loves the renovation. Some of the Shakers who lived here have reincarnated. Some of them have lost interest in this. Ezra is saying there are sixteen Shaker spirits who lived here back then who now return in spirit just to be with the land, to enjoy and to protect it.

They have a very strong relationship with the nature kingdoms here. A number of the Shakers were very clairaudient, clairsentient, and could communicate with the nature spirits. They believed in living in harmony with nature, similar to the Native Americans. They had the same reverence to live in harmony with all of God's creatures. I saw an Indian Chief in full headdress and he was a spirit guide to Ezra at the time. The chief was a brother when Ezra was a Native American.

Tombstone of Shaker Ezra Sherman, Whitewater Shaker Village, Ohio. *Photo by Thomas Freese.*

Ezra studied a little bit about the Mormons and Christianity. He did have some issues with Christianity which is why he started this community. He didn't have anything against Jesus Christ but it was the religious attitudes of some of the Christians which he had trouble with.

Ezra was never married. When he was younger, he had a sweetheart. It ended when she died. He found his path when he was about 36 years old. He was not as good a builder as some of the rest of them. When he was looking for people to have a community with, he looked for others who had those skills. One of his favorite foods was apple butter. They also did a lot of bread baking and sometimes they would make it in the fireplace. I'm getting that the fireplace here in the Meeting House was not the original fireplace. They had a way of cooking bread, kind of a corn bread which they baked in skillets. Sometimes they cooked it here when they were having a party.

They ate deer and they grew their own vegetables although there was some trade. They did some carpentry as exchange for food. There were neighbors here who had a lot of goodwill toward them. These people knew how to do energy work. They were healers. And they did healings on each other, not just through prayer but actual energy work, laying on of hands. Ezra was quite a healer. He had a very strong central channel, a very strong higher line. And just by being around him others attuned to him energetically.

I'm seeing very deep sadness over a two-year old that died of chicken pox or measles or something. That was big trauma. But, in general, there was a lot of good health. But he is telling me that they had a lot of trouble with their teeth. There was nobody to treat teeth so that was sadness for them. There was some stomach and intestinal stuff that killed a few of them, a few died from hard work issues, but generally they lived very long.

He mentions that a lot of the Shaker graves are covered by modern neighborhood homes, and actually, there are graves here that have been built on. He said I wouldn't find the grave of that little child who died.

Ezra had a checkerboard game, just like regular checkers that he liked to play. So they would make those wooden checkerboard games sometimes. He liked to play it more than anyone else. Not that many people were interested in playing checkers with him. They weren't big on that kind of thing. They had pieces of wood that they would toss to each other so it was kind of a "catch" game. They had team races where they would pass a piece of wood to each other. They liked Halloween but they didn't dress up. They liked pumpkins and they liked carving the pumpkins and putting the candles inside. They enjoyed the whole idea of Halloween. They celebrated Christmas and Thanksgiving. Thanksgiving was a big deal for them. It was a major, major thing. They would spend a week in preparation.

They also had sheep and some of the women were able to get wool from the sheep. Ezra looked for women who knew how to do that when he recruited for new members so they could be kept in fabric and new clothes. But a lot of their clothes were also purchased. They brought clothes along when they came to the Shaker community. There was no rule about prohibiting any particular kinds of material.

I'm seeing pictures of the women washing children in tubs outside in nice weather. So they loved being outside. There was a lot of scrubbing. I don't think they had a whole lot of children. It was mostly adults here. I only see three children who came with families. I'm not seeing married couples here but rather everybody single. There was only one married couple who came here and the female died shortly after getting here.

Thomas and Ann walked out from the Meeting House to look at other outbuildings on the former Shaker property.

They used to like to eat out here in the covered area without the walls. They would eat out here when the weather was nice but rainy. Ezra is telling me that they ate these wild violets. They would mix them in with their vegetables. He also says that they had honeybees. Some of them knew beekeeping and that it was nice to have honey. They would go somewhere nearby to buy groceries they didn't have, like sugar and flour, stuff like that. They grew corn. They tried to grow cotton but that didn't work really well. Ezra really wanted the cotton to work out!

Here in the basement they would make butter and separate the milk from the cream. They had one particular recipe for making cheese and they stuck with that. There was a birth that happened here. One woman joined who had lost her husband. She was pregnant when she joined the Shakers. They brought her here for the birth, partly because of the privacy and because it was separated. It seemed like a good place where enough women could get in to attend to her without interference from anyone else. It was quiet and away from the hubbub of the rest of the village. That was the two-year-old who later died.

They didn't have pigs all the time but they had some. Here is the chicken coop. They had *lots* of chickens. They kept the chickens really well fed. The chickens were really healthy and they produced a lot for them. So this was a big contribution to the food supply. They were able to produce enough chickens to sell to surrounding farmers. That was part of their trade. So this was a pretty happy henhouse.

Ezra is telling me about one incident when a fox got into the chicken house and killed a few of them, but since then, they pretty well staked it out and made sure it didn't happen again. They had outhouses back here that are no longer standing.

They used this building as a smokehouse and to dry herbs as well.

When they had a cow or horse die, they would use the hide. They had a couple of people skilled in tanning the hides. They made a lot of belts and that was part of their trade with the community. There was some attempt to make saddles but they were not good at that.

Ezra said they had apple trees, but it seems they died out. Their orchards did really, really well. They had peach and plum trees, too. He said it was because of the way they lived in harmony with the nature kingdom. They had really good produce. Most of the orchard harvest they consumed themselves. They sold a little bit of apple butter to the community.

This section was from the upstairs in the Meeting House attic.

The women danced up here when they wanted to dance by themselves, just women, no men. There were a few teenagers who liked to hang out up here. They had a lot of good storytellers. There was a lot of talent telling tales. That's how they entertained each other.

They did not make glass but bought it from German-descent glassmakers in the Cincinnati area. For things that they could not do themselves, they relied on the German-American community.

Ann and Thomas went next to the Family Dwelling. Ann sees the angled windows.

There is a lot of happy energy at this house. There is joy and a lot of good times here. It was a pretty harmonious group. They had a good sense of humor. There was a lot of playfulness and teasing. There were a number of them who really enjoyed playing practical jokes on each other, not mean jokes but just teasing.

They made some soap. When they had pigs, they used the pig fat and an herb or flower in abundance. [Thomas suggested soapwort to which Ann agreed.]

This was a favorite storytelling place here. They would hang out and tell stories to each other. I'm seeing the women knitting and crocheting when the stories were exchanged. Sometimes they bought yarn and sometimes they had their own. They didn't do a lot of dyeing of fabrics so if they wanted something colorful they would trade. There was some sleeping in these two rooms. This room was for guests.

They fed the wild birds; the sparrows, robins, and starlings, blue jays, and cardinals were all fed when they could.

Spirit Threw Rocks

Postscript on the Information From Ann, Psychic

On the day of Ann's visit to White Water, when we took a break to have lunch, we were sitting in the first-floor kitchen of the North Family Dwelling, next to the Meeting House. As we chatted, I kept hearing the sound of small rocks hitting the floor. It sounded like someone, somewhere was throwing a bit of small gravel, little rocks. I kept looking at the floor and then I asked a few others if they heard the sound, too. They did, and we could not explain what we heard, but it seemed very likely to be from a paranormal source. After our visit, when I got home to Louisville, I emailed Ann to see what she thought about that odd activity, as it seemed at variance from the Shakers more lofty, spiritual-minded activity.

Ann said:

The negative being is a male who is very much damaged, in a lot of pain and very angry that he has been so hurt. He needs a LOT of healing. I haven't sent him off yet, just talked about getting some healing. I may talk with him for a while and if he's okay with it, I'll turn him over to the angels for healing. He was the one who was throwing things when we were at the table. He really wanted attention.

The male from White Water is being attended to. He was pretty much a loner, and a kind of a criminal. He had gotten into several knife fights and had been shot at least three times that I could see. He dressed in black a lot—not solid like Johnny Cash, but close to it. He came to the Shakers to find a safe place to be. He didn't really embrace the Shaker religion, but gave it enough effort to get by. The Shakers took him in and pretty much let him be. He came and went. He never got good medical care for his many wounds, got infections that affected his lungs, which is what he died of. He had left the community, gotten into another scrape and was on his way back when he died. Not a happy guy. His spirit came back to the Shakers because that was the only place he knew where he wouldn't be hurt again.

On the way to the Shaker village, we passed a three-story white building that Lois said was a Shaker building. That building had a whole bunch of souls hanging out there. They were mostly on the top floor. [This is probably the Trustees Office building.]

I have dyscalculia. I get numbers mixed up all the time and I'm really lousy at math and getting phone numbers right. So, don't take any of the years I gave you as gospel. It might have been interesting to channel some of the women. We could have gotten different information and a different perspective.

I met Ann Richer at a psychic fair in northern Kentucky and I was impressed with her friendliness and skill at bringing accurate information from the Source. Ann is a spiritual counselor, working in this field since 1986. She also is a teacher, healer, and spiritual consultant. Ann has seen energies, communicated with the spirit world, and performed energy healings since childhood. She currently teaches classes, conducts private sessions, and is a public speaker on a variety of spiritual arts topics.

As I had invited a few psychics to Pleasant Hill, back in 1998, I only thought it fair to invite one to join with me on a visit to White Water. I felt that the impressions provided by the psychics about the Shakers and Pleasant Hill, were very accurate. I had not briefed either one to tell them about the Shakers and their customs. Likewise, with Ann Richer, I made a point to only tell her that we were driving to an historic location where I would like to record on audio cassette whatever she might pick up.

I arranged with my friend Lois Madden to go along with her to both pick up Ann Richer from her home (in an area of Cincinnati with which I was not familiar) and to lead us from there to White Water, outside of Cincinnati. Lois was going anyway to White Water to join in a volunteer spring cleaning. So on May 6, 2009, Lois, Ann, Jackie, and I arrived at White Water on a beautiful spring day. While Lois swept, helping clean up—she is a member of the Friends of White Water—we met other volunteers and Jackie wandered around to take photographs. I stayed close to Ann to hear what she would say about the Shakers and White Water.

Even though Ann knew next to nothing about the Shakers, I was amazed at how the information she provided dovetailed with both the accurate background I knew of the Shakers and matched very closely with the psychic walkthrough at Pleasant Hill, in Kentucky, eleven years before and from different psychics. Some of these consistent themes for the Shakers are:

- Non-aggressive response to ill thinking or bad treatment in their environment,
- Respect for and cooperative engagement with Nature,
- Playfulness with each other (within their social mores),
- Inventiveness and practicality,
- Interest in a spirituality that encompassed a balance of right living and fervent spiritual worship,
- Connection with Native Americans and their spirits,
- Emphasis on cleanliness and healthy nutrition
- Love of story and song

Without these psychic visits to the Shaker villages, we have only presumptive observations from old journal entries or flitting and mysterious encounters with their ghostly presence.

The Shaker Experience

When I strive to explain the happenings at Pleasant Hill and at White Water Shaker villages, I can't separate the spirit phenomena there from the plethora of ghost tales that are experienced in the greater world. The belief structure of the Shakers must be taken into consideration, but in the end, one must tackle the universal questions of life, death, and spiritual realities. For me, the Shaker ghost stories also occurred in the personal framework of my intimate experience with the Shaker singers, and with the deaths of some family and friends during the years from 1996 to 2001. We lost several Shaker singers who were believers in the spirit occurrences. In attempting to understand the framework of the ghostly experiences that people had, I not only interviewed those who were willing, but also I heard the opinions of the skeptics. Some of those skeptics had worked years at Shakertown and claimed to

Shaker man works on a box.
Courtesy of the Library of Congress.

having seen no ghosts at all. I invited three psychics to visit Pleasant Hill and we walked through the village and about the land. Ultimately, like most of life, our experience at Pleasant Hill may be somewhat projective—we find what we believe, we experience what we already know.

I feel encouraged by hearing from others that they have had their Shaker experiences. In my world view, I believe that people's essence is saved, not destroyed, at death. The spirit is active and often desires to communicate values, thoughts, feelings, and love itself from beyond the grave.

The devotional power of love transforms lives—and according to the Bible—has brought the dead back to life. If our thoughts determine our reality, then look at the sayings and beliefs of the United Society of Believers in Christ's Second Appearing. The Shakers believed that heaven had united with earth. They were living and breathing the reality of Christ returned and of the Millennium.

Love fills my heart and hope my breast
With joy I yield my breath.
'Tis love that drives my chariot wheels,
And death must yield to love."
Shaker Jemima Blanchard, 1845

The Shakers believed that they did not need a priestly class. The Spirit of God and His inspiring agencies spoke directly to them.

> That divinely vitalized beings possess a corresponding power I have not the smallest doubt. Indeed, I have the most undoubted assurance that all such, whether in or out of the body, possess that power.
>
> Shaker Daniel Frazer, 1880

The Shakers allowed and respected spiritual mediums among their ranks. The Shakers were entranced, "slain in the spirit," channeled prophecy and words of wisdom, were given spirit instruments, and received songs and music from a spiritual source. It is certainly possible that the Shaker work world was a direct spiritual gift, including the inspiration for their inventions. They saw visions and angels. Mother Ann performed miraculous healings.

> When we know that mediumistic spiritualism is only the development of a natural faculty,
> The same as singing or speaking, We assign it to its legitimate place.
>
> Shaker Elder Benjamin Dunlavy, 1884

The Shakers applied a clarity and discipline of mind and body to their assumption that the Spirit of Wisdom was the core organizing factor of their lives. Without a clutter of personal possessions and having relinquished sexual attachments, the Shakers were free to live their cherished mental ideals of love and service.

> The spirit world is a world of causes; thus, of effects.
> *Mind* is the primal cause of all material existence.
> Our physical being is in every way subservient to the spirit that animates it...
>
> Anonymous Shaker

The Shakers thus saw little differentiation between the world of matter and the domain of heavenly spirit. All of the life that they were co-creating with divine spirit, was united in the overriding presence of God's freely given love.

> The material worlds! The spiritual worlds!
> Why, is it all not *all* spirit, in different stages of unfoldment...?
>
> *The Shaker*, 1841

With the spirit world ever present and at times hardly discernible from mortal involvement, the Shakers had clearly constructed a Zion, heaven on earth. Why leave Zion, or why not return after the passage we refer to as death? As they opened channels of energy to the greater spiritual world, perhaps they were creating the means for their own spirits to return, by those same energy circuits. The Shakers would then return to be the guardians of a sacred place and spiritual retreat.

> Let thirsty, hungry, starving Zion so live and labor,
> And they will have the key to unlock the heavens,
> And draw from her sacred fountains blessings
> To the satisfaction of every heaven-born soul.
>
> The Shaker Manifesto, 1881

Could it be that the spirits at Shakertown are real and act in our current time and dimension and have an independent, though cooperative, volition? In other words, we seek them and they seek us and we meet as we are able. Many of the Shaker ghost stories from Pleasant Hill point out common experiential attitude adjustments. For instance, there was an employee who was a skeptic and became a believer in ghosts through numerous experiences. Those who might have needed a boost of spiritual faith heard beautiful and inspirational singing. One woman insists she saw an angel, who exhorted the virtues of the Shaker Way. Randy Folger tried "ghost busting" and *he* was busted, in the Whirlwind story! Why would a Shaker spirit grab a hold of a guest in their bed? Maybe they, and only they, knew what the message might have been, like interpreting a dream for our life only. The guardian of the graveyard could have been trying to steer the three young men straight with a little well-timed boost of fear. Or perhaps the Shaker spirits are simply proof that we continue to live past death. We pick up over there precisely where we leave from here.

The Shakers were witness to visions of other people and other worlds. Here is an account from a Shaker community in North Carolina.

Account of a Vision Seen in a Shaker Community in North Carolina, September 15, 1806.

The following is an account of an extraordinary phenomenon that appeared to a number of people, in the county of Rutherford, North Carolina. The report was made the 7th of August 1806, in the presence of David Dickie Esq. of the county and state aforesaid. Jesse Anderson and the Reverend Geo. Newton of the county of Buncombe and Miss Betsy Newton of the state of Georgia who unanimously agreed with the consent of the relations that Mr. Newton should communicate it to Mr. Gales editor of the Raleigh register and state *Gazette*.

Patsy Reaves, a widow woman who lives near the Appalachian mountain, declared that on the 31st day of July last about 6 o'clock p.m., her daughter, Elizabeth, about 8 years old, was in the cotton field about ten poles from the dwelling house which stands by computation six furlongs from the chimney mountain and that Elizabeth told her brother, Morgan, age 11 years, that there was a man on the mountain. Morgan was incredulous at first, but the little girl affirmed it and said she saw him rolling rocks or picking up sticks, adding that she saw a heap of people. Morgan then went to the place where she was, and calling out that he saw a thousand or ten thousand things flying in the air; on which Polly, daughter of Mrs. Reaves, aged 14 years, with a Negro woman ran to the children and called Mrs. Reaves to see what a sight yonder was. Mrs. Reaves said she went about 2 poles toward them, and without any sensible alarm or fright, she turned toward Chimney Mountain. She discovered a very numerous crowd of beings resembling the humans. But she could not discern any particular members of the human body or distinction of the sexes. They were of every size from the tallest men down to the least infants, that there were more of the small than of the full-grown, that they were all clad with brilliant white raiment, but could not describe any form of their raiment, that they appeared to rise off the mountain, south of said rock and about as high, that a considerable part of the mountain's top was visible about this shining host. They moved in a northern direction and collected about the Chimney Rock when all but a few had reached said rock, two seemed to rise together and behind them about two feet a third rose, these moved with great agility towards the crowd and had the nearest resemblance of men of any before seen. While beholding these three her eyes were attracted by three more rising nearly from the same place and moving swiftly in the same order and direction, after these several others rose and went towards the rock.

During this view, which all the spectators thought lasted upwards of an hour she sent for Mr. Robert Siercy who did not come at first, on a second message sent about fifteen minutes after the first, Mr. Siercy came and being now before us he gives the following, relation to the substance of which Mrs. Reaves agrees. Mr. Siercy said, when he was coming he expected to see nothing extraordinary but when come, being asked if she saw these people on the mountain, he answered no. But on looking a second time he said he saw more glittering white appearances of human kind that ever he had seen of men at any general review, that they were of all sizes from that of men to infants that they moved in throngs around a large rock not far from chimney rock, and moved in a semicircular course between him and the rock and so passed on in a southern course between him and the mountain, to the place where Mrs. Reaves says they rose, and that two of a full size went before the general crowd about twenty yards and as they respectively came to this place they vanished out of sight disappeared. Leaving a solemn and pleasing impression on the mind accompanied with a diminution of bodily strength.

Whether the above be accountable on philosophical principles or whether it be a prelude to the descent of the holy city I leave to the impartially curious to judge.

G. Newton

On the same evening and at the same time several miles distant from the above place there was seen a bright rainbow apparently near the sun then in the west where there was neither the appearance of clouds nor haze in the atmosphere.

An Interview with Shaker Scholar Carol Medlicott

Carol Medlicott teaches cultural and historical geography at Northern Kentucky University. She researches the Shaker west and Shaker music, and her work has been widely published. Carol began her research on Shakers in 2004 with a post-doctoral fellowship in New Hampshire, during which she became more closely acquainted with Shaker history through the New Hampshire Shaker sites. She is active with the Friends of White Water Shaker Village and the Western Shaker Singers.

How would you describe the spirituality of the Shakers and how might it connect with people's contemporary search for spiritual meaning?

That's a tough question! Answering it requires one to generalize thousands of people, spanning some twenty villages over a thousand miles and some 230 years! But I would say that one theme common across the whole gamut would be that Shakers saw their spirituality as an integral part of their everyday life, not something they indulged in on Sabbath or at worship meetings, but something that imbued everything they did. The idea was to try to free themselves from the shackles of biological family ties, sexuality, materialism, etc., so that they could better experience that constant spirituality. Shakers really were like a monastic order. Remember that Thomas Merton, the twentieth-century Trappist monk and philosopher from Kentucky, really idealized Shakers, but just how deeply he probed Shaker history is not too clear. One wonders whether he focused on a few idealized notions about Shaker spirituality and overlooked a lot of historical details. I think there is a tendency for a lot of people to do that. So that's just something to be aware of.

How were the Ohio Shakers unique within Shakerism?

Ohio Shakers had a reputation for exuberance, and for somewhat unconventional interpretations of Shaker life. Easterners were placed in powerful positions in both Ohio and Kentucky, and it was not until the latter half of the nineteenth century that either Ohio or Kentucky Shakers fully ran their own show, so to speak. At the height of the Shaker movement, the Ohio Shaker population probably exceeded that in pretty much any other state, except New York.

Thus, it's been woefully overlooked, relative to the rest of the Shaker world. With the exception of a few early transplanted Easterners, no Ohio Shaker ever saw Mother Ann or any of the founding generation. So it's no surprise that they would put their own "spin" on the faith. White Water is a particularly interesting site, as it remained very spiritually vigorous longer than other sites, east or west. Shakers at White Water were still attracting local audiences for their singing, dancing, and preaching long after other Shaker sites had become more staid and subdued.

How do you feel when visiting the old Shaker places?

It depends. For the most part, I feel a sense of friendliness and benevolence. The extensive restorations and museum displays of places like Pleasant Hill make it seem less "Shaker" to me, more like a sterile museum space. For me, less is more, in terms of the historic preservation process.

In what ways was Shaker song significant in their worship and now, for us, with our current ways of relating to them?

Shaker music hasn't gotten its due attention, relative to the Shakers' other categories of creative output. Shakers were about spirituality, first and foremost—not chairs, not buildings, not baskets, not garden seeds, not oval boxes. Spirituality was grounded in worship, and Shaker worship was virtually impossible without music. So what was the significance of music for worship? It was everything! Shaker sites, in my opinion, don't do nearly enough to emphasize that.

Many years ago, in the mid 1990s, I had a moment of epiphany when listening to a Shaker music CD that hearing their music would help put me in the heads of the Shakers of the past. I still feel that way. But I feel like it's difficult to do that, because we lack the numbers of people, the spontaneity, the exuberance, and the sheer volume necessary to experience music the way Shakers would have experienced it in meeting. I think the decibel level of a large shape-note singing is more on par with what Shaker meeting would have been like. Or it would even be like the "glory and praise" singing of a big evangelical church. Yet, the typical visitor to a Shaker site might hear a lone interpreter singing, or might hear a CD playing gently in the background of the gift shop, sounding ethereal and angelic. That may be appealing, but it's not representative of how most Shakers experienced music.

I recently wrote a book chapter on music, which appeared in a volume called *Inspired Innovations: A Celebration of Shaker Ingenuity*, by Steve Miller, published in 2010 by University Press of New England. My chapter is called "Innovations in Music and Song," and it focuses on this very question. In general, I think that it's difficult for us modern folks to connect with the music of the past, because we hold it up to the lens of our own contemporary aesthetic sensibilities, what we consider appealing or not. Some of the Shaker music genres are more palatable than others.

Shaker sister Alice Smith extends her hands to receive God's blessings. *Courtesy of the Library of Congress.*

For certain, most modern folks lack the patience to fully appreciate Shaker hymns and hymn lyrics. Moderns simply don't have the attention span for 12 or 16 or 20 verse hymn, even though that hymn will teach them something about Shaker spirituality. Anthems, too, are a hard go for moderns, but the Shakers wrote hundreds and hundreds of them. Short dance songs from the 1840s seem to be the most easily translatable to the contemporary ear. Obviously, *"Simple Gifts"* is in that category. But that genre of music is just the tip of the iceberg.

Why do you think the Shaker spirits might be active at the old villages?

The Shakers didn't have a sense that heaven was somewhere else, up in the sky, whatever. They already regarded the space of a Shaker village as "Zion." So in death, they expected to remain in Zion, but simply on a different plane. At least, that's my understanding for the pre-Civil War period, speaking in very general terms. I'm less familiar with how Shaker attitudes about death and spirituality transformed later on. I think they believed that there was something sacred about the spaces of their "Zion," so for that reason I would not be surprised at the notion of Shaker spirits remaining.

Can you provide some journal information of communication the Shakers had with their brethren after death?

There is SO MUCH of this sort of thing! Letters, journal references, margin notes in hymnals. If folks can spend some time with some primary sources, then this will give you a better sense of how "natural" it was for the Shakers to interact with the spirits of those who had passed. One place to start is with hymnals from the 1838-1850 period. They are replete with margin references to songs being brought by specifically named Shakers who had passed, by people who came into their midst bringing songs and other gifts. It seems that some of the living members of the community were more gifted seers than others, and could more readily recognize and identify the visiting spirits. There are extensive accounts of spirit sightings in some Western Reserve materials, some in the Ohio Historical Society in Columbus.

The period of 1838 to 1850 has come to be known among Shaker scholars as the "Era of Manifestations," because the interaction with spirits was almost constant. Each community had mediums and seers, who both experienced visions and interpreted the visions of others. Many of the spirit manifestations during that period were angelic beings, Biblical figures, and a range of famous historical figures. Others were spirits of Native Americans or people of other races—Chinese, Pacific Islanders, and so on. And still others were specific Shakers, some who had passed recently and others who had passed many years before.

Here is one interesting example. At Union Village, Ohio, a young man from one of the early convert families, named Andrew Houston, was clearly being groomed for leadership as he grew to adulthood. He was sent east for a visit in the 1820s, and by the early 1840s it was clear that he would soon assume an important leadership role. Sadly, things changed very suddenly in 1844. That fall, the Union Village Shakers were constructing their large new brick dwelling house (the one that was torn down, ironically, by the management at the Otterbein Home). Andrew Houston was working high up on the scaffolding, and somehow he fell from the attic level to the ground. He died within a few hours. That was on October 7th, 1844. Within a few weeks, Andrew Houston's spirit appeared at both Union Village and nearby White Water bringing songs and messages. I have transcribed and sung those songs. And another interesting part of the story is that last year I found a journal entry by a Union Village Shaker sister describing a dream that she had foretelling Andrew Houston's death. She reported that in the dream, she saw a large black object falling from the scaffolding of the new dwelling; it frightened her, and she knew that it was Andrew Houston falling to his death. I can't explain this, except to say that I believe there were Shakers who had legitimate gifts of insight and prophesy. And did Andrew Houston's spirit really bring those songs a few weeks after his death? Clearly, the Shakers believed that, and saw nothing particularly peculiar about it.

Last year I ran across an interesting account by a Shaker sister at Union Village who clearly seemed to be describing what we would call a "ghost." It was an apparition of a Shaker who had recently passed, but instead of this spirit bringing messages for the group, he seemed to be trying to speak with one living Shaker who was sitting there, oblivious to the spirit's presence. In other words, only the sister could see the spirit and the others in the room were unaware of him. She saw the same spirit the next day, moving through the streets of the village, trying to communicate the message that he had for the living Shaker. She wrote that she initially intended to keep the information to herself, but after telling an Eldress, she was instructed to write down the experience, because what she had seen was genuine.

I have also seen evidence that the Shakers believed that they could project their spirits into distant places, visiting other villages, and so on. Here's one example. A beloved teenage member of White Water, Ohio, a young girl named Hannah Agnew, was sent to live at New Lebanon, New York in 1836. A couple of months after she had arrived, a New Lebanon journal records that an evening gathering of Shakers was visited by a spirit from White Water, who had come to see how Sister Hannah was getting along, and would take a report back to Ohio that she was well and happy. The Shakers took things like this in stride and it was just part of their everyday reality.

I would like to mention one final example, which I encountered in Shaker sources. Around 1840, a young female medium from Union Village was instructed by the Elders to travel in spirit to New Lebanon, New York. This was to be a test of her abilities. She had never been to New Lebanon, but the Elders had, and they questioned her about the details of the buildings, the fences, etc. She evidently passed the test. The Elders decided to send her a second time, this time with a specific errand of reading a document that the Union Village Elders wanted to see. This time, the young medium reported that a fearsome dark figure chased her all the way back to Ohio. She was so terrified that she flatly refused to do any more spiritual traveling.

I am grateful to Carol Medlicott, who discovered this letter in her research at the Winterthur Library and brought it to my attention.

Detail of a letter by Shaker Andrew C. Houston to Austin Beckingham, March 21, 1839. *Courtesy, The Winterthur Library: The Edward Deming Andrews Memorial Shaker Collection.*

Shaker Leader is Near

Carol Medlicott continues her discussion:

At Victory of Light psychic fair in Sharonville, Ohio, I was in a packed session of "group readings" with four psychic readers in turn. It started out so-so, the kinds of readings that skeptics pounce on. You know what I mean, I'm sure. Such as, "I'm getting a 'B'. Does a 'B' name mean anything to anyone?" And this was in a room full of 150 people. What use is that?

Anyway, the final psychic reader was talking and was almost done. She paused and said she was getting one more thing that was really important. She walked up the center aisle to my row. I was sitting about four people in from the center, wearing a pink sweater.

She pointed right at me, and said, "For you in the pink sweater, there is an older man standing behind you with his hands on your shoulders."

She went on to describe him—lively and witty, old-fashioned clothing, a visible tremor, receding hairline. She said he wanted me to know that I have plenty of time, that things will get finished in time. She said he would not leave my side, and that was what drew her up the aisle, that he drew her closer.

So of course this sounds exactly like Issachar Bates, and does NOT really sound like any ancestor that I'm aware of. Bates did have a visible tremor. He was lively and witty, etc. So that seemed pretty remarkable to me. Maybe he is hanging with me after all. I've often wondered.

Conclusion

The phenomenon of the Shaker spirits, as they appear in our lives, is a four-way intersection where Shaker history, spiritual communication, mind operating beyond space and time, and our journey through mundane activities, intersect. With an initial examination, it would appear that ghosts, in general, could be souls or energy stuck here on earth. And thus would not encounters with Shaker ghosts be an indication that many Shakers, like ghosts in the rest of our world, are unable to move out of the dimension of their eternal present, or what we would refer to as the past? Perhaps—and particularly as we see them enact daily routines, such as walking familiar paths, engaging in work, and hovering over their buildings and land.

Yet there are many nuances which seem to suggest that the Shakers are present in a way that is more dynamically interactive with our lives and the circumstances in which we come to their village. That is, the Shaker spirits do often seem to respond to who we are as unique personalities, what we are doing in the particular moment of now time, and how often they can even still teach us about kindness and a gentle place in the world. Furthermore, the transcripts from psychics seem to indicate conversations and interactions with much more than the wisp of a remnant of a former person. Indeed, the Shakers appear to, having shed the gross body, be free to worship, sing, praise, work, and offer fellowship to anyone who comes to their realm in earnest and heartfelt intent. And through what could be called accident or perhaps by a mysterious synchronicity that might be called Divine luck, many individuals have had life-altering experiences with the Shakers-in-spirit. I have no doubt that the relatively small number of stories that meandered into this collection represents a fraction of the ghost or spirit encounters at Shaker villages in America.

Seeking evidence of, or experience with, the Shaker spirits is a quest dissimilar to the quick and cheap fascination with the dead, as seen on television shows or in stereotyped stories in movies and books. This should not be another stop in the bus tour of interesting haunts of the dead. True, the Shakers were mortal and lived and died, like others now known as spirits or ghosts. But the Shakers lived for the spirit world, lived in the spirit world, and moved freely back and forth between the two. If you could be slain in the spirit and lie prone for twenty-four hours, if you saw the dead and chatted with them, if you got direct revelations and inspiration to sing and dance and pray in tongues... then, you were a Shaker. And that is a totally different kind of spirit both before and after that momentary adjustment in existence which we call death.

I believe that a Shaker spirit, different from your ordinary house ghost, if you will, is a teaching spirit, a high-minded soul, and a ghost that is not sad and earthbound, but delights in those who come seeking spiritual truth. So my advice is to go ahead and seek! Get thee to a Shaker village, walk their paths, see their homes, be inspired by their sacred architecture, read about their lives and tragedies and triumphs. Listen to Shaker music, take a class and learn to make a set of nesting wood, swallowtail boxes. Sing their songs and plant an herb garden like they did. And perhaps, if you have something to learn, and they have something to teach, then you will have a Shaker experience, whether that is simply being joyful while hearing "Simple Gifts" or feeling a wonderful peace while sitting on a bench in the Meeting House, or receiving a "gift" to twirl and laugh. That the Shakers well knew how to live in this life surely commends to their mastery of the spirit world too.

Cedar tree and Water
House, Pleasant Hill.
Photo by Thomas

Readings and References

Andrews, Edward-Deming, *The Gift to be Simple*. Dover, NY: Dover Publications Inc., 1962.

Bauer, Cheryl & Rob Portman, *Wisdom's Paradise: The Forgotten Shakers of Union Village*. Wilmington, OH: Orange Frazier Press, 2004.

Baute, Paschal, *"Storytelling Mystery, Power and Genius: How Storytelling Nurtures the Human Spirit."* www.paschalbaute. com.

Bial, Raymond, *Shaker Home*. Boston, MA: Houghton Mifflin Co., 1994.

Boice, Martha, Covington, Dale & Spence, Richard, *Maps of the Shaker West: A Journey of Discovery, A Collection of Maps and Histories of Better Known Shaker Sites in Kentucky, Ohio, Indiana, Illinois, and Michigan, Beginning in 1800*. Dayton, OH: Knot Garden Press, 1997.

Boles, John B., *The Great Revival: Beginnings of the Bible Belt*. Lexington, KY: University of Kentucky Press, 1972.

Boles, John B., *The Great Revival, 1787-1805, The Origin of the Southern Evangelical Mind*. Lexington, KY: University Press of Kentucky, 1972.

"South Union's Shaker Cemetery Re-discovered." *Bowling Green Daily News*, April 12, 2011.

Brewer, Priscilla J., *Shaker Communities: Shaker Lives*. Hanover, MA: University Press of New England, 1986.

Byrnside Burress, Marjorie, *White Water Ohio Village of Shakers, 1824-1916: Its History and People*. Cincinnati, OH: Reprinted through Friends of White Water Shaker Village, Inc., 1979.

Cimprich, Vickie, *Pretty Mother's Home: A Shakeress Daybook*. Frankfort, KY: Broadstone Books, 2007.

Clark, Thomas D., *Pleasant Hill in the Civil War*. Lexington, KY: Pleasant Hill Press, 1972.

Clark, Thomas D. & Ham, F. Gerald, *Pleasant Hill and Its Shakers*. Harrodsburg, KY: Pleasant Hill Press, 1968.

Cleveland, Catherine, *The Great Revival in the West, 1797-1805*. Chicago, IL: University of Chicago Press, 1916.

Cohen, Joel, *Simple Gifts: Shaker Chants and Spirituals*. New Gloucester, ME: Shakers of Sabbathday Lake, Schola Cantorum, 1995.

Conklin, Paul K., *Cane Ridge: America's Pentecost*. Madison, WI: University of Wisconsin Press, 1990.

Eads, Harvey L., *Shaker Sermons: Scripto-Rational. Containing the Substance of Shaker Theology Together With Replies and Criticisms, Logically Set Forth*. Cambridge, MA: Harvard College Library, the Bequest of Evert Jansen Wendell, 1918.

Emlen, Robert P., *Shaker Village Views*. Hanover, NH: University Press of New England, 1987.

Eslinger, Ellen, *Citizens of Zion: The Social Origins of Camp Meeting Revivalism*. Knoxville, TN: University of Tennessee Press, 1999.

Faber, Doris, *The Perfect Life: The Shakers in America*. New York, NY: Farrar, Strauss & Giroux, 1974.

Freese, Thomas, *Shaker Ghost Stories from Pleasant Hill, Kentucky*. Bloomington, IN: AuthorHouse, 2005.

Freese, Thomas, "Shaker Ghost Stories from Pleasant Hill, KY". Lexington, KY: *Chevy Chaser Magazine*, Vol. 2, No. 11, November, 1998.

Greene, Nancy Lewis, *Ye Olde Shaker Bells*. Lexington, KY: Transylvania Printing Co., 1930.

Hewlett, Jennifer & Kocher, Greg, "Two Mercer County Men Die in Collision on U. S. 68". Lexington, KY: *Lexington Herald Leader*, July 3, 1999.

Horsham, Michael, *Shaker Style: A Celebration of the Beautiful Workmanship of the Shaker Movement*. Hertfordshire, England: Eagle Editions, 1989.

Johnson, Lee, *The Struggle for Watervliet, Ohio*. Washington, D.C.: SpiritTree Press, 1999.

Klamkin, Marian, *Shaker Folk Art & Industries*. New York, NY: Dodd, Mead & Co., 1972.

Maclean, J. P. & Franklin, Burt, *A Bibliography of Shaker Literature*. New York, NY: Lenox Hill, 1905.

MacLean, John Patterson, *Shakers of Ohio*. Columbus, OH: F. J. Heer Printing Co., 1907.

Marty, Martin & Micah, *When True Simplicity is Gained: Finding Spiritual Clarity in a Complex World*. Grand Rapids, MI: William B. Eerdsmans Publishing Co., 1998.

Mastin, Bettye Lee, *A Walking Tour of Shakertown*. Lexington, KY: Richard S. Decamp, 1969.

McNemar, Richard, *The Kentucky Revival or A Short History of the Late Extraordinary Outpouring of the Spirit of God in the Western States of America*. New York, NY: Edward O. Jenkins, 1886.

Merton, Thomas, *Seeking Paradise: The Spirit of the Shakers*. Edited by Paul M. Pearson, Maryknoll, NY: Orbis Books, 2003.

Morse, Flo, *The Shakers and The World's People*. New York, NY: Dodd, Mead & Co., 1980.

Morse, Flo, *The Story of the Shakers*. Woodstock, VT: The Countryman Press, 1986.

Neal, Julia, *The Shaker Image*. Hancock, MA: Shaker Community Inc., 1974.

O'Keefe, Nancy &. Randolph, Sallie G., *Shaker Inventions*. New York, NY: Walker and Co., 1990.

Patterson, Daniel, *The Shaker Spiritual*. Mineola, NY: Dover Publications, 2000.

Phillips, Hazel Spencer, *Richard the Shaker, Shaker Bicentennial 1774-1974*. Lebanon, OH: Warren County Historical Society, 1972.

Phillips, Hazel Spencer, *Shakers in the West*. Philadelphia Museum of Art, PA: Spring Reprint from the Philadelphia Museum Bulletin, 1962.

Pope, Richard Martin, *Cane Ridge and the Shakers*. Paris, KY: Cane Ridge Bulletin, Vol. 4, No. 3, April 1971.

Promey, Sally B., *Spiritual Spectacles: Vision and Image in Mid-Nineteenth Century Shakerism*. Indianapolis, IN: Indiana University Press, 1993.

Provensen, Alice & Martin, *A Peaceable Kingdom: The Shaker ABCEDEARIUS*. New York, NY: Viking Press 1978.

Ray, Mary Lyn, *Shaker Boy*. San Diego, CA: Browndeer Press, 1994.

Richmond, Colin Becket, *A Collection of Shaker Thoughts*. Oneida, NY: Richmond Colin Becket, 1976.

Stechler Burns, Amy & Burns, Ken, *The Shakers: Hands to Work, Hearts to God*. New York, NY: Portland House, 1987.

Stein, Stephen J., *The Shaker Experience in America: A History of the United Society of Believers*. New Haven, CT: Yale University Press, 1992.

Stepp, Holly E., "Shakers' Secret Site of Worship is Found." Lexington, KY: Lexington Herald Leader, April 14, 1998.

Thomas, Samuel W. & James C., *The Simple Spirit—A Pictorial Study of the Shaker Community at Pleasant Hill, Kentucky*. Harrodsburg, KY: Pleasant Hill Press, 1973.

Thorne-Thomsen, Kathleen, *Shaker Children*. Chicago, IL: Chicago Review Press, Inc., 1996.

Turner, Ann, *Shaker Hearts*. New York, NY: Harper Collins, 1997.

Turner, Rosalind, "Unsolved Mysteries Abound at Shaker Village." Harrodsburg, KY: The Harrodsburg Herald, July 16, 1998.

White, Anna & Taylor, Leila S., *Shakerism Its Meaning and Message: Embracing an Historical Account, Statement of Belief and Spiritual Experience of the Church from Its Rise to the Present Day*. Columbus, OH: Fred J. Heer Press, 1905.

Whitson, Robley Edward, *The Shakers: Two Centuries of Spiritual Reflection*. Ramsey, NJ: Paulist Press, 1983.

Yolen, Jane, *Simple Gifts: The Story of the Shakers*. New York, NY: The Viking Press, 1976.

Other Books by the Author

Fog Swirler and 11 Other Ghost Stories. Bloomington, Indiana: AuthorHouse, 2006.

Ghosts, Spirits and Angels: True Tales from Kentucky and Beyond. Morley, Missouri: Acclaim Press, 2009.

Haunted Battlefields of the South. Atglen, Pennsylvania: Schiffer Publishing, 2010.

How to Make Southwest Jewelry in Wood. Atglen, Pennsylvania: Schiffer Publishing, 2010.

More True Tales of Ghosts, Spirits and Angels. Morley, Missouri: Acclaim Press, 2011.

Shaker Ghost Stories from Pleasant Hill, Kentucky. Bloomington, Indiana: AuthorHouse, 2005.

Sometimes Life Ain't Sweet, You Know, (as illustrator), Shirley Hayden-Whitley. Lexington, Kentucky: I. B. Bold Publications Co., 1994.

Strange and Wonderful Things: A Collection of Ghost Stories with Special Appearances by Witches and Other Bizarre Creatures. Baltimore, Maryland: PublishAmerica, 2008.

The King Determined to Die (El Rey Resuelto a Morir). Louisville, Kentucky: Illumination Publications, 2010.

www.ThomasLFreese.com

Index

Photographs